APPLIED CREATIVITY

Your guide to revolutionary thinking

and the six skills to unlock your creative potential

Christopher S. Sellers

Published by Christopher S. Sellers

Sydney, Australia

Copyright © Christopher S. Sellers 2022

Cover design: Travis Hinkle & Christopher S. Sellers

Layout: Christopher S. Sellers

Editor: Jessica Stewart

Printed in Australia by Ingram Spark.

Sellers, Christopher S.

ISBN print: 978-0-6456332-0-7

ISBN ebook: 978-0-6456332-1-4

ISBN audiobook: 978-0-6456332-2-1

Disclaimer

The material in this publication is of the nature of general comment only and does not represent professional advice. It is not intended to provide specific guidance for any particular circumstances and it should not be relied upon for any decision to take action or not to take action on any matter which it covers. Readers should obtain professional advice where appropriate, before making any such decision. To the maximum extent permitted by law, the author and publisher disclaim all responsibility and liability to any person, arising directly or indirectly from any person taking or not taking action based on the information in this book.

Where appropriate names, details and locations have been changed to preserve privacy and confidentiality.

"Christopher has changed my mind about creativity with his beautifully written book; challenging and practical, he demonstrates the awesome value of creativity, inviting the reader into the process.
Creativity is not someone else's domain, its available to you too, Chris has shown me how and I am so glad he did".

Sharee Johnson - Psychologist & Executive Coach, SKJ Consulting
Author of *'The Thriving Doctor'*

"This book hooks you in from the start. Balanced and well researched, Christopher provides deep insight into qualities we all possess, and ignore at our peril.
Ranging from spies to entrepreneurs the story telling is superb.
This is a book you should keep close, to remind yourself of the potential reward, rather than than the challenge - of embracing creativity".

Matt Milloy - Film-maker & BBC Producer, mattmilloy.com

"Creativity is a tricky word to define, a tricky concept to wrap the head around. I've probably put more time into understanding creativity than most, and I've been blown away by how thoroughly Christopher has translated creativity into a usable framework".

Tony Albrecht - Creative Director at CONTENDER
Author of *'In the Creative Arena'*

"Christopher has introduced an exciting, original approach; providing us with the means and resources to engage productively. Innovation becomes a meaningful and valuable result rather than just a topic of discussion".

Adrian Jobson - Founder & Principal Consultant, Acculture

"The simplicity of the six creative skill sets has changed how I think about strategy. In his book 'Applied Creativity', Christopher provides a practical framework that leaders can apply to increase their performance by harnessing the power of creativity"

Robert Andersson - CEO Nutri-Pharm (Australia)
Author of *'Who Makes a Leader Not What'*.

Dedicated to the Magicians, the Muses and the Masters;
(may you find yours).

Christopher S. Sellers

Introduction   1

1. The Hotel Room   7

  i: Candidate #7   8

  ii: Disruption   13

  iii: Hacks   18

  iv: 'God does not play dice'   28

  v: Six Creative Skill Sets   34

2. The language of creativity   37

  i: Aristotle and Architects   38

  ii: Rouge vs. Gold   44

  iii: Productivity   50

  iv: Latin   58

  v: Renaissance   64

3. Collaboration vs. Creativity   67

  i: Inspiration   68

  ii: Candour   74

  iii: Echo chambers   82

  iv: The individual   89

  v: Prolific. Proactive. Leading. Original   95

4. Emotions + Risk: why we avoid creativity   101

    i: I can't draw…   102

    ii: Risk   108

    iii: Emotions   112

    iv: The Arts   123

    v: Failure   134

5. Six Creative Skill Sets   141

    Welcome to Rouge 101   142

    1. Problem-solving   145

    2. Innovation   151

    3. Composition   157

    4. Adaptability   161

    5. Emotional intelligence   167

    6. Originality   171

Conclusion   177

The reveal   183

Contacts + Resources   189

Acknowledgements   195

About the Author   199

Introduction

I'm going to show you a magic trick.

First, I'm going to demonstrate the impossible...

I'm going to define creativity for you; what it is, why you think it, why you feel it, how it behaves and how it applies to you and everyone around you.

Second, I'm not going to hide the method.

I'm going to demonstrate how this magic trick is done.

Finally, while attempting the impossible and exposing how it's done, I'm still going to blow your mind.

By the end of this book, you too will be a creative genius and capable of extraordinary magic!

Sounds impossible? Don't believe me? Perfect. Creativity has a habit of defying belief to produce the exceptional.

Like all good stories, we should start at the beginning...

It started when I dropped out of uni, to live and train in a kung fu school. My parents weren't happy, they were concerned about my future. Secretly auditioning for acting college probably didn't help either; and from there it was all downhill...

Acting and writing for theatre and screen, street photography, travelling to London, I didn't land my first 'real job' until I was 25 —by this stage I had already worked in a cabaret lounge, acted in a few short films, been a private eye for a week (wild story), and optioned two television concepts: one to the BBC, the other to a new online movie service, something called Netflix?

I describe the next fifteen years as 'hopscotch between corporate and creative': juggling tech start-ups, WB films, designing L&D assessments, performing fringe theatre and founding production companies.

Then a pandemic arrived and all of a sudden creativity was hot. Not just hot... critical.

Standard process failed. Standard thinking stalled. Employees refused to return to the office. Crypto and NFT's rose and burst. War erupted in Europe. Recessions loomed. Unprecedented times required unprecedented thinking... one would think.

In 2022, a report by the World Economic Forum (WEC) cited the 'Top 10 Skills Required by 2025'—skills like innovation, complex problem-solving, originality and ideation.
Basically, creativity.

But the second half of the article is where things take a turn—the WEC offers how we should develop our creativity and issues a shopping list of technical skills: content writing, sales, marketing, data entry, AI, cloud computing and engineering.
To the WEC, creativity is defined by its relevance to corporate and STEM... and nothing else.
Equally concerning is the logic that technical skills can develop creativity—a logic we've seen play out (and fail) in education, at every level, everywhere, for the last two hundred years.

It is curious to me that those seeking creativity ignore fields where creative skills, intelligence, process and outcomes are demonstrable, abundant and replicable.
Basically, the arts.

When we use the word 'creative' we immediately associate it with the arts: your ability to draw, dance, sing or act, seems to define whether or not you are creative.
Artists are known to be radical thinkers who thrive on inspiration and are capable of extraordinary feats; to an artist, the corporate discussion of 'creativity' makes as much sense as an opera ensemble discussing financial accounting.

It is as if corporate and the arts,

speak two very different languages.

Both insisting they know what creativity is,

both dismissing the other as irrelevant.

I wondered… what if these languages were the same?
That these are two villages whose inhabitants settled either side
of a river, who were raised to believe that 'them on the other side
is weird'.
This book is your bridge between two worlds—a creativity
translator, of sorts—leading you to a brighter, creative future.

The benefit of having such a diverse career is that it has allowed
me to observe, teach and practise creativity in work, education
and life, across many different fields.
It also helps that I'm a trained, professional creative with a diverse
body of work behind me: theatre, screenplays, street
photography, blog articles, film/video, the occasional card trick
and even writing this book… rather than being a casual fan of
creativity or an academic studying a foreign process.

What I've found is creativity is less a formula to produce
'magic'—more a language to be learned.

Everyone speaks a little; fluency requires skill, knowledge and application. Like any language, you can learn it, we can objectively measure it and begin to apply it immediately. However, like any language, you also need others who understand you—if there is one trait synonymous with creativity, it's that creatives, creative process and creative ideas are more often misunderstood, invalidated, dismissed or feared.

In this book I'm going to show you:

- Where the current demand for creativity came from and why.

- What you observe as creativity is driven by six specific skill sets.

- The key to optimal creative process lies in you, the individual.

- Why you avoid your own creativity and how to overcome risk.

- A comprehensive breakdown of the Six Creative Skill Sets and how they apply to you.

My goal is to demonstrate that creativity is grander, far more rich and potent than currently defined. At the same time, I'll dismiss the mysticism and elitism that often clouds creative process. I'll detail the pitfalls and misconceptions of creativity and the thinking that has led us here.

By the end of this book you will have a crystal clear understanding of exactly what creativity is, what creative strengths you already possess and actionable steps to develop these skills for yourself.

I applaud you for being here, this isn't for the faint of heart and I'm here to challenge much of what you believe to be true… that's a creative's job.

What better place to start than a hotel room in regional Australia.

1. The Hotel Room

i: Candidate #7

One Thursday afternoon on a military training facility in regional Australia, nine intelligence candidates sat in a waiting room in a small, residential complex. That afternoon was their final trial, a live operational scenario dubbed 'the Hotel Room'.

Candidate #7 (C7) was a female, in her twenties. She wore black jeans, a grey singlet, sneakers, her hair pulled back into a ponytail. Called to the hotel room, **C7** wiped her palms against her jeans as she approached the Assessor outside the hotel room door. The Assessor read her the brief...

ASSESSOR: This is a hotel room. Somewhere within the hotel room there is an Easter egg; it looks like this...
(*holds up a bright orange USB key*).
Once you enter, you have three minutes to find the Easter egg. After three minutes, bad guys arrive. Once bad guys arrive, you have sixty seconds to escape the room. If you have fail to escape the room within this sixty seconds, you lose. You're dead. Any questions?

C7: How many bad guys?

ASSESSOR: We don't have that information.

C7: *(pointing to the USB key)* Can I have that to match against the one I find?

ASSESSOR: There's only one, there are no duplicates. Ready?
(C7 nods and enters the room)
(The Assessor closes the door behind her and starts the timer)

Inside the hotel room is a queen bed with a bedside table either side, a telephone and an alarm clock hosted on each. There's an empty wardrobe with coat-hangers, a small coffee table, a bar fridge, a television, and a small ensuite bathroom with basic linens.

On the surface, the hotel room appears to be an elaborate Easter egg hunt, so let's play along and see if you can solve it.
The conditions are fairly simple:

1. You're in a hotel room.
2. Find the Easter egg.
3. Bad guys arrive in three minutes.

C7 starts by assessing the layout of the room then begins to search in a clockwise manner: first the wardrobe, then the bar fridge, she moves the coffee table out of the way to check underneath the bed, then rifles through the bedsheets.

C7 unplugs the phone and pockets a pen before finding the Easter egg in the drawer of the bedside table.

The Easter egg was preset in the same place for all the candidates.
Some found it faster. Some slower. A few didn't find it.
Let's say you found the Easter egg too, congratulations.
How did you compare? How long did it take? Does it matter?
You found the Easter egg. If you leave now, you can escape before bad guys arrive.
Problem solved.

You walk to the door and turn the handle—the door is locked.
This is not what you expected. You're trapped inside the hotel room and cannot escape. What are you going to do?
Bad guys are coming soon. When?
How long ago did you enter and how are you keeping time?

Is this something you accommodated for or did you start searching through the wardrobe?

If you remain calm and walk through the steps, you can probably find a solution:

1. You're locked in a hotel room.
2. Find the Easter egg? / You've found the Easter egg? / Ignore the Easter egg?
3. Bad guys will arrive ~~in three minutes~~ … imminently.

If you recall, there was one last condition:

4. 'Once bad guys arrive, you have sixty seconds to escape from the room.'

There's your window, how are you going to use that sixty seconds to escape? At times like these, it is often helpful for the moderator to give you a tip…

Standard process for operatives is to break down engagements into three responses:

1. You can run.
2. You can hide.
3. You can fight.

C7 is in the bathroom doing her hair.

Three minutes is up…
Bad guys enter.

Sixty seconds…
What are you going to do?
Run… hide… fight… something else?

Thirty seconds…
Bad guys aren't speaking and they aren't moving.

Ten seconds…

In the time it has taken you to read this, **C7** has safely escaped the Hotel Room.

Time's up.
You're dead.

ii: Disruption

For many, the Hotel Room feels like a Kobayashi Maru—an unsolvable puzzle, a rigged game where the house cheats to win. For these candidates, the Hotel Room was designed to simulate a world where the rules no longer apply, standard process has failed, they must **adapt**... or die.

You died.

Surely a trained candidate stands a better chance of surviving? This is where the results of the Hotel Room get interesting.

Over 90% of trained candidates failed the Hotel Room: they all died, an unprecedented outcome. Imagine your product suffering a 90% recall, or if your team was found to be operating at 10% efficiency.

On this Thursday, **C7** was the only candidate to pass the Hotel Room; she wasn't any more skilled than her peers, she had exactly the same information and she didn't cheat.

What's more remarkable, is that **C7** achieved an optimal outcome.

She didn't just 'pass'... she achieved the best possible outcome, in the best possible manner, in the fastest recorded time.

So how did she do it?

Was she exceptional, lucky, naturally creative or all of the above?

Before we answer that, it might be worthwhile to ask, why does this matter? Why was the Hotel Room designed, what were they looking to find and how is it relevant to you?

*

The Hotel Room simulates 'disruption'.

When standard process fails... how do you flex your creativity to adapt, solve, innovate... survive?

Whether a global pandemic, a competitor launching a new app, the rise and fall of crypto, or some other crisis—disruption is a cause and effect. You are either the disruptor or the disrupted. What is sobering to realise is that disruption is not new.

Pandemic: COVID19. AIDS. Ebola. Zika. SARS. Bird flu.

Conflict: Terrorist attacks. World wars. Civil wars.

Financial: GFC's. Financial depressions. Crypto bubbles.

Social/environmental: Natural disasters. Black Swan anomalies.

Personal: Relationship break-ups. Death. Divorce. Betrayal.

Once we recognise that change/disruption has always existed, that it will continue to occur, that it may manifest anywhere, at any time, in any form and is unlikely to be predictable, there are some serious questions we should ask.

How well do you cope **emotionally** with change?
How well can you **solve problems, adapt** and **innovate**?
How well do you **compose original** outcomes to lead?

This is what the Hotel Room set out to demonstrate and where we find unique insight into creative thinking, skills, process and outcomes.
This was an organisation which operated in a fluid world of change; even so, they understood that they could provide the base level of training for candidates to competently operate. I call this Linear Expertise.

Every industry has its own version of Linear Expertise: fundamental knowledge and skills required to competently fulfil a role. Harvard Professor, Teresa Amabile refers to this as 'domain skills' in her Componential Theory of Creativity.

Doctors must understand chemistry and biology to accurately diagnose patients.

Architects must understand math and geometry to calculate dimension and design your apartment.

Actors must understand dialogue and be physically fit to perform Shakespeare in the round.

For this organisation, they believed their training and process to be sound and the Hotel Room was an attempt to assess the creative skills outside of their Linear Expertise.

How would candidates **emotionally** respond to panic?

Could they **adapt** to changing conditions?

Could they dynamically **problem-solve** challenges?

Could they independently **innovate** their own process?

As the only survivor of the Hotel Room, perhaps there is some insight we can draw from **C7**—her creative thinking, process and outcome. What did she do differently that allowed her to survive where everyone else around her failed and died?

Her solution may surprise you...

Bad guys enter.

Sixty seconds remaining.

C7 is standing at the foot of the bed, folding a towel, her hair is neatly pinned up with a pen.

C7: *[Addressing the BAD GUYS]* Good afternoon gentlemen, I apologise. I must have mistaken your check-in time. It seems you'll require more towels. I'll be right back.

C7 places the folded towel on the bed, walks through the bad guys and exits the room.

Eighteen seconds.

iii: Hacks

Looks simple, doesn't it? I call this the Magic Trick Paradox.

Ever seen a card trick that blew your mind?

Somehow a magician pulls your card from their pocket where moments ago you had seen it in the middle of the deck... it defies physics and common sense.

It is an impossible feat. This was magic. They're an incredible magician.

However, if our magician was to walk us through their process, you'd realise that a double-lift is one of the most simple and most prolific sleights any amateur magician may perform. Once demonstrated, the illusion evaporates and the solution appears elementary.

It was a basic technique. It was not magic. They're not special.

So too with the Hotel Room; a solution, once demonstrated, appears rudimentary.

Locked in a hotel room = Pretend to be staff

This is the Magic Trick Paradox and this mode of observational thinking, plagues creative outcomes everywhere, seriously diminishing the appreciation of both Linear Expertise and Creative Intelligence.

Though the solution for the Hotel Room appears to be simple, two pages ago, you could not see it, you did not solve it, you died.

To observe the outcome and to believe... 'It's so simple, anyone could do that'... is an art critics logic. The cynic who visits the gallery and mocks the Pollock or Warhol, though they, themselves, have not painted a thing.

Secondly, observing only the outcome is a dangerous trap which promotes 'hacks'. If someone else has done the work, it seems savvy to copy them. As a by-product, we often bypass in-depth research, critical thought and context in order to Google search someone else's quick solution.

Solving problems with hacks ignores the Linear Expertise it requires to arrive at a solution, while also bypassing creative thinking, skills and process.

This prompts a more serious consideration of Creative Intelligence; observing **C7's** solution, is it really that creative?

Could you tell the difference between a hack and genuinely creative solution?

Standard thinking says 'no'— common opinion insists creativity is completely subjective, relative and impossible to measure— however the Hotel Room demonstrates how you might critically evaluate creative outcomes.

There are two keys to surviving the Hotel Room:

1. One requires Linear Expertise: base skills/knowledge acquired by trained **Professionals**.

2. One requires Creative Intelligence: a combination of Six Creative Skill Sets.

For this breakdown, I'll refer to candidates with Linear Expertise as **Professionals**, and those of us without as **Amateurs**.

*

The first key to solving the Hotel Room is the locked door, which requires Linear Expertise. Amateurs feel the locked door is unfair and point to it as the reason they failed.

'You never told me the door was locked, doors don't lock from the outside!'

This is where most of us die; we pursue our goal then suddenly encounter an unforeseen obstacle, the rules crumble, standard process fails and our best laid plans disintegrate. When disrupted and forced to **adapt**, **Amateurs** panic, blame the conditions and guess at solutions.

For **Professionals** entering the Hotel Room, checking the door was step number one. Assessing potential exits, for an intelligence candidate, is as elementary as a double-lift to a magician. It is a simple, effective, learned technique that, with practice, becomes seamless second nature. **C7** applied a basic technique to identify a detail that reframed the conditions of the Hotel Room.

Amateurs	Professionals
I'm in a hotel room	I'm locked in a hotel room
Find the Easter egg	I've three minutes to plan an exit
Bad guys arrive in three minutes	I have one minute to execute

For **Professionals**, the Easter egg becomes a secondary priority to not dying; a significantly different landscape to our **Amateur** perspective.

The second key to the Hotel Room is your exit, which requires Creative Intelligence. Like all good puzzles, the information you need to **solve** the Hotel Room exists within the puzzle itself; in fact a solution is offered to you in the very first sentence of the brief.

'This is a hotel room...'

What kind of people frequent hotel rooms?
Generally there are two types:

GUESTS or STAFF

This insight isn't new, you just didn't immediately recognise it.
Now it seems obvious.
Another magic trick.

A candidate's **emotional intelligence** would allow them to interpret foreign context and place themselves within this context —in doing so, discover two potential **solutions**: you could adopt the role of either GUESTS or STAFF.

This insight enabled **C7** to **adapt** and **compose** a specific **solution** to survive.

Walking through the breakdown, we may wonder if a solution appears so simple, why did so many Professionals fail? We could assume a lack of creativity; this solution seems to require a level of abstract or lateral thought, normally reserved for artists and savants. The truth is less esoteric.

The Hotel Room exposes a unique cognitive blindspot.

For **Amateurs**, the scenario appears as an 'Easter egg hunt' and while we may creatively improvise a hack, we lack the expertise to effectively manage the conditions.

For **Professionals**, candidates would enter the Hotel Room, identify the condition of the locked door and default to Linear Expertise as standard process:

1. **Run**: The door is locked.
2. **Hide**: Failure to exit in sixty seconds results in 'death'.
3. **Fight**: Engaging an unknown number of threats, within a room you could not escape was deemed non-viable.

Linear Expertise provides foundation for competency however, within disruption, when these systems fail, adherence to standard process more often compounds the issue. Could these candidates think and act outside their training? In times of disruption, when systems fail and people panic, can you?

For both the **Amateur** and the **Professional**, the Hotel Room appears increasingly rigged to fail. (Secretly) locked doors, non-viable process, Easter eggs that are red herrings, it is unfair, broken, messy, cheating, inconsistent and impossible.

If this is true, how did **C7** survive?

With the same information, within the same parameters, how do some individuals manage to see what no-one else could to create the exceptional and **solve** the impossible?

The challenge is not what you think…but how.

As **Amateurs** we can only rely on our creativity since we lack an informed or experienced opinion.

As **Professionals** we often prioritise our Linear Expertise, relegating our Creative Intelligence.

In a disruptive landscape, where the 'rules no longer apply', discovering creative solutions to impossible situations are the golden insights every industry is seeking to harness.

Ideally, we wold seek to utilise both.

LINEAR + CREATIVE = OPTIMAL OUTCOMES

What allowed **C7** to survive was that she was the only candidate to align her Linear Expertise with Creative Intelligence to achieve an optimal outcome.

Here's everything you don't see...

C7 enters the hotel room and assesses the door is locked; this allows her to panic early and affords her the maximum amount of time to adapt and prioritise objectives.

She uses the alarm clock by the bed to structure her time, allowing two minutes to find the Easter egg, after which she would ditch her search and focus on her exit.

While searching, **C7** finds the Easter egg and proactively mitigates threats: she rearranges the coffee table to the middle of the room, pockets a pen and unplugs the phone from the wall, in case she needs them as weapons.

In the bathroom, **C7** rolls the Easter egg into her hair, pulls it into a bun and skewers it in place with the pen. She explained it would look more fitting for STAFF and she wanted her hands free and hair up in case she needed to engage.

C7 removes a towel from the bathroom and begins to remake the bed. Bad guys enter to see a girl standing at the foot of the bed, folding a towel.

C7 addresses the bad guys, proactively taking control of the situation, offers an explanation, then takes action. Bad guys see no reason to prevent her; within context, why would they?

C7 exits the Hotel Room with the Easter egg, untouched, in eighteen seconds.

Can you see the difference? Which would you prefer? To die? A hack? Or an optimal outcome? You can also begin to see how you may objectively evaluate Creative Intelligence.

Now, here's your disclaimer… not all of us deal with such high-risk scenarios; human life is seldom on the line and the consequences of poor choices are more likely a missed opportunity, a disappointed client or a failed project. Secondly, our avenues for creativity are usually restricted to a casual instrument or polite hobby, they are not so rigidly assessed.

Here's where you're accountable... why not?

If creativity is a requirement, how do you intend to identify, train and measure creative skills, including vet creative thinking, process and the outcomes they deliver?

The demand for creativity to **solve** complex **problems**, drive **innovation**, foster **emotional intelligence**, **compose** new products and generate **original** ideas has spawned a slew of gimmicks, philosophies, hacks, tips and tricks (we'll look at some in the next few chapters).

When there is a demand for creativity to improve how you live, work and learn, perhaps it is time to critically evaluate what creativity is, how it behaves and how you can practically apply it.

There is one last lesson we can draw from the Hotel Room, one last trick hidden from the casual observer.

This disruption was not an accident—it was an assessment specifically designed to evaluate the creative potential of candidates in a specialist field. They met 'disruption' and they had been exposed—their process failed, thinking failed, training failed and the outcomes were unacceptable.

Someone broke their process, a radical genius who could 'think outside the box'... a civilian, of all things... an actor.

iv: 'God does not play dice'

I am not a spy.

I would not pass an aptitude test. I have an allergic reaction to authority and the feedback from my psychological profile determined I was 'unsuitable'.

At the time I was as a contract L&D designer and I'd turned my acting/screenwriting experience to designing role-play scenarios for government HR assessments. To me, role-play scenarios were short scenes with a twist: you had characters/candidates with respective needs who had to overcome conflict to reach a resolution.

Acting had taught me how to interpret other characters' mindsets and emotions. Screenwriting had taught me how to articulate these needs within the context of a scene.

When I was initially approached by this organisation, it was to design a scenario to assess creative problem-solving.

The brief allowed four weeks to compose an assessment to evaluate core competencies (ie. their Linear Expertise), as for the creative problem to be solved, that was up to me.

Scepticism was high… what could a civilian with no military background possibly teach them?

I did myself no favours when I replied after two days...

'I'm ready. We'll need an apartment with some basic items.'
'Do you have a budget for expenses?'
'Oh, like $50.'

Curiosity was piqued when the first testing instructor died.
Curiosity twisted to concerned interest when the majority of candidates died.
So how did I do it?
How did I beat spies at their own game?
As mentioned earlier, the Hotel Room reflects the principle of disruption. If the standard process for these candidates is to Run, Hide, Fight, I thought...

'What happens when standard process isn't viable?'

In a disruptive environment when 'the rules' no longer apply—could a candidate think outside their training?
I composed a scene that reflected this; the candidates were my characters, I walked them through several scenarios that might simulate these conditions. I folded in the core competencies to be assessed. I crafted context and story around their situation.

The alarm clock, phone, pens, coat-hangers and towels were all strategic props, including the Easter egg, the threat of bad guys and locking the door from the outside. Just like a film scene, everything you see is by design—everything has a purpose and a place.

Finally, what creates a scene? Characters, conflict and a story. This made up the candidate brief.

"You need to find a thing in this room. Bad guys are coming. You need to get out alive".

Two days in design was supported by ten years of **professional** creative process, writing, editing, performance and production. I was proud of what I had created. It was a cool concept in a really interesting field. On the day of testing, I was nervous to prove myself and excited to see the results.

I did not expect everyone to die.

In any other industry, a fail rate of more than 30% would suggest the exam is 'too hard'—fault would not lie with the candidates or the organisation— it would be mine. To my relief, this was exactly what these trainers were looking for: blindspots in their process. This perspective is what set their leadership apart from most organisations—weaknesses exposed strengths to be developed.

But it was in the debrief for the Hotel Room where everything changed for me. Identifying why candidates had failed wasn't enough; it is vague to say someone lacks creativity and the assessors challenged me to explain... 'How do we fix it'?

How can we practically develop creative thinking and skills and apply them to what we do?

And to be honest, I didn't know.

For most artists, creative process is personal, abstract and mostly intuitive, but here I was attempting to explain to military folks how I created an impossible card trick and how they could do it for themselves.

There was one key distinction I made first—that one process was **proactive** and one was **reactive**.

The Hotel Room had been created **proactively**, similarly to an artist creating work to put out into the world: there was a brief or an idea and something **original** was **composed** to achieve a goal.

C7's process was **reactive**: she was subject to this disruption and was forced to **adapt** and **innovate** in order to find a **solution**.

Both processes require creativity, but there was something more. Like Einstein, I tend to believe that 'God does not play dice'... Meaning, rather than random magic that strikes everyone differently, I felt that creativity could abide a universal logic and cohesive set of rules.

That's when I identified something interesting...

I designed a **problem**...
C7 solved a problem.

I **innovated** existing process...
C7 innovated her training.

I **composed** a scene with props, conditions and story...
C7 composed her role as STAFF.

I **adapted** screenwriting technique to design the Hotel Room...
C7 adapted to disruption.

I applied **E.Q** to place myself in the context of the puzzle...
C7 applied **E.Q** to interpret context in her solution.

I designed an **original** scenario...
C7 designed an **original** solution.

The goal of the Hotel Room was not to 'break' anyone's process, rather it was to ask—can we distil the skills that make up creative thinking, process and outcomes?

Though our professions could not be more different, what **C7** and I had in common is we each applied Six Creative Skill Sets in harmony with our Linear Expertise to achieve an optimal outcome.

If these skills can be identified, they can be taught, learned, assessed and improved—this organisation now had six tangible skills they could develop.

Creativity was not esoteric philosophy; it was practical set of skills that were measurable and immediately adoptable.

v: Six Creative Skill Sets

The silver lining with all disruptions is that when something fails, you are gifted an opportunity to improve it.

Skills like **problem-solving** and **innovation** allow you to overcome challenges and improve existing systems and process.

Your ability to interpret context and empathise with changing needs requires a level of **emotional intelligence** if you're going to **adapt** effectively.

Perhaps you recognise it's more strategic to be proactive, to move ahead of the curve and **compose solutions** that are forward-thinking, sustainable and mitigate risks.

Your ability to conceive of **original** ideas, solutions and outcomes is what will define your 'key point of difference' and establish you as a leader in your field.

Proactive or reactive the Six Creative Skill Sets are universal.

Mechanics **problem-solve** as often as corporate strategists.

YouTubers **innovate** as often as engineers.

Musicians **compose** as often as UX designers.

Dancers **adapt** as often as military operatives.

Counsellors employ **emotional intelligence** as often as artists.

And all are capable of delivering **original** ideas in their field.

Rather than applying one skill, independently, in isolation, perhaps you identify the value in all of these skills and recognise that they are versatile, that they complement and enhance each other. In an ideal world, you might like to employ all of these traits, imagine what could be possible?

There is one last creative step I would ask you to take with me, one that offers you a quantum leap in potential. This is where I show you how all magic tricks are done.

Often, when we talk of creativity, we observe inspiring works of art, incredible **solutions** to impossible problems, astonishing **emotional** performances, revolutionary ideas that change the world.

We observe the outcome and try to work backwards to comprehend the process. We observe the **output**… which is like observing the illusion.

The true untapped potential of creativity lies in your ability to apply these Six Creative Skill Sets to **input**, to how you learn, to how you interpret and process information, to how you proactively conceive of ideas.

Applying the Six Creative Skill Sets to your own Linear Expertise, is what allows you to 'think outside your training' and deliver optimal ideas, solutions and outcomes.

*

In the debrief I asked **C7** how she recognised this scene as a hotel room and why she chose to role-play as a maid?

'Oh, I used to work in hotel reception, this kind of thing happens all the time.'

She wasn't exceptional. She was a highly skilled professional who aligned her Linear Expertise with Creative Intelligence... and she'd seen this card trick before.

2.

The language

of creativity

i: Aristotle and Architects

Once upon a time in Greece, circa 350 B.C, Aristotle's demonstrated range of knowledge included biology, botany, chemistry, ethics, history, metaphysics, rhetoric, physics, poetics, political theory, and psychology. He pioneered the study of zoology and was the founder of formal logic.

One fateful day, Aristotle was summoned by King Philip II of Macedonia, to act as tutor to his 13-year-old son and heir, Alexander. Within twenty years, Alexander had conquered most of the known world as skilled strategist, General and politician, earning him the moniker 'the Great'.

Alexander the Great founded more than twenty cities that bore his name, most notably Alexandria in Egypt, many of which became major cultural centres surviving up until the 21st century. As a ruler, Alexander allowed conquered societies to retain their religious and political institutions, going against his tutor's belief that it was right to keep non-Greeks as slaves.

Alexander was erudite; he patronised both the arts and sciences, he had natural charisma which made him a great leader, and was also reported to be an excellent dancer.

When we review the cradle of education, whether the Greeks, Mesopotamians or Romans, we find language, philosophy and art were of parallel import as math, science and politics.

There was an understanding that these subjects harmonised and enhanced each other, the culture was one of curiosity; open critique was encouraged, the goal of education was to produce wise, well-rounded citizens.

*

Nowadays, when we use the word 'creative', we think of temperamental artists—erratic, emotional, capable of extraordinary feats, though impossible to manage.

It seems we can't reliably employ creative process, unlike mathematic or scientific formulas.

It's a talent, not a skill; creative outcomes can't be quantified or validated like economics or law.

Those who wield creativity appear to possess mystical gifts; whether it be raw talent, divine inspiration, luck, psychological chemistry or a combination of all of the above.

We therefore throw creativity into the arts bin and there it remains:

CREATIVITY = ARTISTS ONLY

This belief seems to be accepted by corporate and creative alike, which creates a bit of an issue…

If creative skill sets are in demand, how might we develop our own creativity? Is the definition of creativity; the act of producing a new and useful thing or is there something more? Are creative traits born, learned, gifted or none of the above?

When practically applied to our lives:

How can we **solve** our own problems more effectively?

How can we **adapt** to crises and **innovate** more successfully?

How can we **compose** new and **original** ideas, products or tools?

In recent history, to answer questions of human behaviour we have turned to the sciences to unpack the hows and whys of what we think and do. However, science and creativity have somewhat of a dysfunctional relationship for as much as the sciences would seek to find order with rational study, creative outcomes often appear random and confusing.

For example, let's say we attempted to assess creativity via a standardised, replicable assessment.

Imagine you gave one floor plan with the same conditions, same timeframe and budget, to five different architects—you will most likely receive five very different home designs.

This is one of the gifts of creative process—the ability to observe the same information, within the same parameters, and draw out a unique result. In business, this trait is of exponential value: when everyone has the same information and resources, creativity allows you to find what others couldn't, **solve** what others didn't, compose what others didn't think possible.

However, within a scientific model of study, this creative insight reads as 'inconsistent'. If the input is standard, the conditions and process are standard, but the outcome is variable, this creative outcome is translated as fault/erratic/risk/outlier.

Consider the two processes..

Standard Linear process:

STANDARD INPUT ⟶ **STANDARD PROCESS** ⟶ **STANDARD OUTCOME**
STANDARD INPUT ⟵ **STANDARD PROCESS** ⟵ **STANDARD OUTCOME**
(correct, accurate, scientific, replicable, productive, beneficial)

Creative process:

STANDARD INPUT ⟶ **STANDARD PROCESS** ⟶ VARIABLE **OUTCOME**
ERROR 404 ⟵ **ERROR 404** ⟵ VARIABLE **OUTCOME**
(random, incorrect, unpredictable, outlier, fault, anomaly, risk)

On a standardised graph, **C7** would be regarded as an anomaly, compared to 90% of her peers.

Another issue lies in that there is no creative stable for science to observe as a baseline.
Architects are not dancers yet each display creative traits and return a random, creative, result—as such, standard models of assessment tend to hit this creative wall.
Creativity does not behave like we expect it should.
Creative process cannot be standardised for a predictable result.
Creativity is random, unmanageable and relies on the individual.

Since science cannot accurately observe creative process, it determines that it must be an individual talent; thus, it endeavours to examine the origin of this process, and turns its attention to the brain. Pop-psychology studies reference creativity in terms of 'neuroplasticity' or 'cognitive flexibility'.

The once popular left brain/right brain model has been supplanted by terms like neurotypical vs. neuroatypical. It is claimed that neurodiverse individuals excel at 'finding unique patterns'… as if we were villagers seeking guidance from the savants of old.

Corporate practice has a love affair with psychological studies: everything from Myers-Briggs, to Type A/Type B, Big Four and Big Five Ocean. Business articles cite neuroscience and clamour for 'cognitive and emotional flexibility' as key personality traits to unlocking potential and leading with empathy.

Despite the best of intentions, scientific and psychological studies reinforce the notion that creativity is predicated entirely on one's genetics. This assertion is not only inaccurate, it is misleading and often dangerous in its implications.

If creative process were purely genetic what if we weren't born atypical? Should we resign ourselves to the notion that the potential to **adapt, solve problems, innovate, emotionally connect** or **compose** anything **original,** remains the gifts of the muses?

In homage to Aristotle, let's apply some basic logic…

ii: Rouge vs. Gold

If creativity were some kind of genetic trait that only savants could conjure, then we could apply this logic to anyone in any creative field, so let us revisit our architects.

Your average architect understands abstract concepts; they possess a sense of symmetry and can visualise a floorpan in 3D.

ARCHITECT = CREATIVE

On the other hand, we recognise your average dancer as creative: inspired by music, colour, form and function, dancers through rhythmic choreography, evoke emotion to tell a story.

DANCER = CREATIVE

If creativity were genetic, and architects and dancers are both creative, would this mean that all architects can dance?

ARCHITECT = CREATIVE
DANCER = CREATIVE
∴ ARCHITECT = DANCER

Unfortunately, no not all architects can dance.

There are core skills and knowledge one must possess in order to be a competent architect or dancer respectively—this is unseen half of the 'gifted creative' myth.

No-one is born a dancer, no more than they are born an architect or a surgeon or mechanic— there are Linear skills one must learn before mastery may be achieved.

What we recognise as creative in our architect are skills of **composition, adaptability** and **originality**. Equally what we recognise in dancers are creative skills of **composition, adaptability** and **originality.**

Understanding that not all architects can dance, yet architects and dancers both demonstrate creative traits, logically we can infer how these skills may be demonstrated in other professions. In doing so we establish a critical creative distinction:

Creativity is not inherent to any type of personality, genetics or profession.

We can see how an architect, applying creative skill sets of **composition, adaptability** and **originality**, may yield a very different result to a dancer, applying the same creative skill sets.

Our architect may design a cutting-edge apartment.

Our dancer may choreograph a dynamic routine for an ensemble.

This is why creative process often appears so confusing to scientific and technical study: attempting to apply a standardised, Linear model of assessment to a personal, abstract process is nonsensical and offers superficial insight.

The scientific language, models and methods we rely on to deconstruct and make sense of our world—while effective in other arenas—are inaccurate tools in recognising and translating creative skills, process and intelligence.

They are, quite simply, the wrong language.

Just as applying English grammar to the French language renders us hapless and confused, to understand creativity we must learn its language.

*

Imagine that creativity was a language, for fun, let's call it Rouge.

CREATIVITY = ROUGE

The good news is you speak Rouge fluently, you always have.
From the tender age of six, you dawdled into school speaking Rouge.
Teachers addressed you in Rouge.
You played in Rouge.
You learned in Rouge.
Each day your fingers were sticky with paint and the alphabet was taught in rhymes.

As you progress through the years, you are gradually weaned off Rouge and instructed in Gold.

LINEAR = GOLD

Teachers now address you in Gold.
All your subjects are in Gold.
You learn Gold to repeat Gold in Golden exams.
You quickly become aware that success is measured only in Gold.
There is no more finger painting and nothing is taught in rhymes.

You remember playing in Rouge and how much fun that was, but your options are diminishing, perhaps a handful of extracurricular activities scattered around your main Golden responsibilities.

Your parents fret over how well you understand Gold. You remind them of your love for Rouge, but they warn Rouge isn't worth as much as Gold.

Gradually your passion for Rouge dwindles; it is exhausting and painful to speak when no-one understands you—indeed a most effective method to teach a language is immersion within its culture.

Over time, Gold has evolved as our dominant language, the Socratic method has been replaced by enclosed institutions with scripted learning—wisdom uncovered through exploration, discussion and play, fails to fit neatly in a text book nor can it be graded against peers on a standardised test.

Our values follow suit.

For most, math, science and English are compulsory subjects, where art, drama and music are hobbies. This trend continues into tertiary education: economics, medicine and law, carry more weight than philosophy, dance or a secondary language. STEM has evolved as the crown jewel in all of education.

Why?

Because education's primary purpose is to skill its students in a singular occupation; as such, creative skills have been dissected, diluted and dismissed in favour of standardised, Linear form-fitting function.

We have strayed far from Aristotle and Alexander.

Once proud, the creative expression of art, music, philosophy, dance, poetry are now deemed of little worth unless there is some direct, tangible, measurable, Golden ROI attached to it.

Of what use is creative thought within a syllabus that requires you only to read, recite and replicate given information, from given sources, in a standard format?

Where should you learn to **solve** complex problems?

What value has **emotional intelligence**?

How have we come to mock **originality** as an ideal to aspire to?

Creativity has been relegated to the Latin of languages: foreign, rarely used, barely valued and practically redundant in modern use.

Like Latin, were creativity a dead language and no longer relevant to society, then this argument is moot. We have evolved, we've shed the unnecessary and should embrace the future. Instead, we find the opposite to be true and the demand for creativity is more desperate now than it ever has been.

iii: Productivity

The current global demand for creativity is a paradoxical scenario; collectively, we are the most intelligent generation that has ever lived. Compulsory public education in the Western world has seen more of its population educated than any generation prior; we are now living in an era where information is global, abundant, immediately accessible and free.

In counterpoint to this age of information, we observe an avalanche of studies demanding the need for creative thinking. Forbes, HBR, LinkedIn, CNBC regularly cite skills such as **innovation, emotional intelligence, problem-solving** and the ability to **adapt**, as critical skills for the future.

On paper, this would seem like the ideal time for creativity to be embraced, so what is this demand?
If we're more educated now than ever—living in the Golden age —where has this demand come from and why?
It doesn't quite make sense, does it?
It's as if the technical skills we have learned, been drilled and valued on, are insufficient.

It's as if standard education and training, cannot and does not deliver creativity… for if it did, surely we would not be here.

As Einstein famously noted, we can rarely **solve** our **problems** with the same thinking that delivered them and I'd suggest that the issue at hand is not one of skills, intelligence or education, rather a problem of language, translation and values.

For the last two hundred years, we have been comprehensively schooled in Gold, while Rouge has been allowed to atrophy in the corner. Our situation appears more grim once we realise that during this Golden era, we have manifested a unique dialect, one that has passively shaped our education, our work, even our relationships—the language of productivity.

*

It is worth examining this term.

The etymology of productive is rooted in the Latin: *Producere - Product* (brought forth). From 1700–1800, the term productiveness was in common use, up until the first Industrial Revolution, when productivity was redefined to mean 'the quality of being productive'.

In 1899, productivity was redefined again as an economic value as 'rate of output per unit'—note that 'unit' does not differentiate between tool, machine, program or human.

This definition, ethic and process has been globally adopted to become the Gold standard for every industry.

So what does this mean for you and why does it matter?

*

Imagine the standard week equals 40 hours and in this time, you are able to complete 40 tasks:

40 TASKS ⟶ 40 HOURS

Imagine you invent a tool that allows you to complete the same amount of tasks in half the time:

40 TASKS ⟶ 20 HRS ······ 40 HOURS

You are now 50% more efficient, however you are simultaneously 50% less productive.

By creating a deficit of 20 hrs, a unit must double its output to maintain optimal productivity.

80 TASKS ⟶ **40 HOURS**

The acceleration of technology and services, while becoming more efficient, is interpreted by 'productivity' as 'potential capacity'. Once we apply this logic, there is no escaping the cycle:

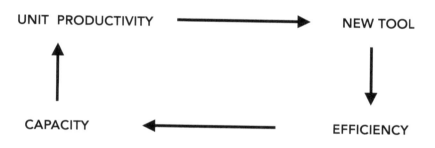

Productivity is a most elegant echo chamber:

- Productivity drives demands for efficiency.
- Demand drives supply for new tools.
- New tools create capacity.
- Units must satisfy capacity to maintain productivity.

This cycle of productivity is as observable for students in education as it is for employees in business.

To maintain productivity, improve systems and restore them when they fail, arguably we require a degree of creativity to enhance services and invent new tools.

Herein lies the disconnect... productivity requires a standardised process to mass produce a standardised outcome.

Creativity within a standardised process often produces a variable outcome... (see our architects).

These two processes are non-compatible.

Gold does not recognise...

Cannot translate...

Does not value...

Rouge.

This inability to translate creative thinking, skills, process and outcomes, is as observable for students in education, as it is for employees in business.

What plays out is a masterclass in language; what is observable in every society, is that a dominant culture will appropriate what it finds valuable and adapt it to fit its understanding.

Since STEM cannot accurately recognise creative thinking nor accurately translate creative outcomes, Gold isolates traits it finds valuable and redefines them as something more palatable.

~~CREATIVITY~~ = INNOVATION = PRODUCTIVITY

It is no coincidence that in recent years STEM has soared in value and propagated a slew of 'design thinking' methodologies in an effort to productively **solve problems** and drive **innovation**—it is Golden thinking for Golden problems and it is as dysfunctional as it sounds.

These advocates are perhaps the furthest removed from Aristotle and Alexander and this siloed approach to creativity and **innovation** has contributed to our current decline, here's why…

A demand implies a deficit.

The commercial demand for **problem-solving** and **innovation** is well-documented, though it is but one symptom of a much darker cancer.

Pandemics drove organisations into a **reactive** pivot, exposing an inability to intelligently **adapt**.

In parallel, we observe an increased demand for **emotional intelligence**—the soft skills required for clearer communication, empathy in leadership, resilient teams and ethical cultures.

The demand for **composition** and **originality** are considered to be fluke occurrences, rather than designed outcomes.

That the cry for creative skill sets is global and systemic cross-industry, should tip you to the notion that something very serious is awry. Slowly the full scope of our situation tilts into focus…

The demand for creativity is driven by three major influences:

1. Productivity devaluing 'non-essential education'.

2. Pandemics disrupting established process.

Though sleeping beneath them all for almost three centuries…

3. A collective lack of creative intelligence.

What Forbes *et al...* unwittingly identify is not a demand for skill sets, rather a deeply established, creative and intellectual deficit compounded by scarcity.

Two hundred years of standardised learning has collectively returned a standardised outcome; we are only now starting to realise we may have shortchanged ourselves.

There are few individuals within their field who are fluent in both Rouge and Gold and no-one speaks Latin anymore.

iv: Latin

Grasping the root of the problem we can better understand how
we have arrived in our current predicament, our demand for
creativity is caused by:

- A lack of creative skills... which we have not learned.
- A lack of creative intelligence... which we have not developed.
- A lack of creative solutions, ideas, products... since we have
  not fostered effective creative process.

In clearly understanding the problem and factors at play, we can
take intelligent steps to address them. If there is a demand for
creativity, how can we develop creativity for ourselves?
I believe this is an issue of language and translation, not genetics,
skills or intelligence. So perhaps we should ask a different
question—how might we learn the language of creativity?

Let's start with the basics...

A B C D E F G H I J K L M N O P Q R S T U V W X Y Z

This alphabet may look familiar but, like many creative outcomes,
appearances may be deceiving.

This is the Latin alphabet standardised circa. 700 ad. Though Latin itself may be a dead language, you may be interested to know that Latin cultivated over seventy derivative languages that are still in active use today.

A B C D E F G H I J K L M N O P Q R S T U V W X Y Z - LATIN

A B C D E F G H I J K L M N O P Q R S T U V W X Y Z - FRENCH

A B C D E F G H I J K L M N O P Q R S T U V W X Y Z - ENGLISH

A B C D E F G H I J K L M N O P Q R S T U V W X Y Z Ä Ö Ü ß - GERMAN

A B C D E F G H I L M N O P Q R S T U V Y Z - ITALIAN

A B C CH D E F G H I J K L LL M N O P Q R RR S T U V W X Y Z - SPANISH

A B C D E F G H I J K L M N O P Q R S T U V W X Y Z Å Ä Ö - SWEDISH

At a glance, these alphabets appear similar and we may attempt to reconcile similarities between them. However, in context, we come to understand they are vastly different and there is little point in attempting to apply English rules to French or Swedish.

A few tips on foreign languages:

- Each language is unique unto its culture and context.
- Each language abides by its own grammar and phonetics.
- Each language may be taught, learned and improved.
- You can identify a beginner from a fluent conversationalist.
- Your ability to become fluent in a language is not dependent on genetics, personality or profession.

Similarly, creativity is the root from which we derive multiple skills.

A B C D E F G H I J K L M N O P Q R S T U V W X Y Z - CREATIVITY

A B C D E F G H I J K L M N O P Q R S T U V W X Y Z - PROBLEM-SOLVING

A B C D E F G H I J K L M N O P Q R S T U V W X Y Z - INNOVATION

A B C D E F G H I J K L M N O P Q R S T U V W X Y Z - COMPOSITION

A B C D E F G H I J K L M N O P Q R S T U V W X Y Z - ADAPTABILITY

A B C D E F G H I J K L M N O P Q R S T U V W X Y Z - EMOTIONAL INTELLIGENCE

A B C D E F G H I J K L M N O P Q R S T U V W X Y Z - ORIGINALITY

At a glance, these skill sets appear similar and we may attempt to reconcile similarities between them. However, in context, we come to understand they are vastly different.

A few tips on creative skills:

- Each skill obeys unique behaviour; proactive/reactive/both.
- Each skill facilitates a different function.
- Each skill may be taught, learned, measured and improved.
- You can identify a basic outcome from an optimal outcome.
- Your ability to become proficient in a skill is not dependent on genetics, personality or profession.

*

I describe creativity as language, more specifically than a 'muscle to exercise'—muscles perform a singular function—a bicep curls to lift things, a tricep extends to release things.

Languages are multi-dimensional.
Languages require an understanding of context and the culture that surrounds them.
Learning a new language often enriches the understanding of your native language.
Learning a new language develops Abstract Intelligence... (more on this later).
Languages are versatile, practical and applicable to the world around them.
Languages require practice, discipline and offer some challenges in application.

This brings us to the root issue of all languages—learning a language requires others who speak and understand us, for without practice it will atrophy and, like Latin, die.
Equally, creativity is dependent on the people and culture around us in order to be spoken, survive and thrive.

What value has **innovation** if the current system is 'good enough'?

We do not create Uber, a platform designed to bypass the standard process. We would not seek new ingredients or methods to cook new and delicious meals.

What value is **composition** if 'functional' is adequate?
We do not create Apple computers; a brand renown for its intuitive OS and iconic design. We cannot paint, photograph, illustrate, dance or write music.

What value is **originality** if 'everything has been done before'?
We will never discover Uber or Apple, nor will we ever aspire to.
We will never be Picasso, Jobs, Nina Simone, Aristotle or Maya Angelou, nor develop the confidence to claim our own authentic personality.
It starts with values.
Valuing all of creativity, rather than only the attributes we assume to be useful or profitable, in doing so, we discover that truly exceptional outcomes, for both corporate and the arts, are possible when we harness the full potential of creative skill sets.

Aligning your Linear expertise with a confluence of creative skill sets, enables **optimal** creative solutions, ideas and outcomes.

LINEAR SKILL SET

+

PROBLEM-SOLVING

INNOVATION

COMPOSITION

ADAPTABILITY

EMOTIONAL INTELLIGENCE

ORIGINALITY

APPLIED CREATIVITY

OPTIMAL thinking, skills, process.

Proactive, prolific, leading outcomes.

v: Renaissance

Here's what we know... we recognise an outdated model of productivity has cultivated unsustainable conditions.

We recognise current models of education are insufficient for modern needs when information is abundant, immediately accessible and free.

We recognise that science and business apply ineffective models to translate creativity, creative thinking, creative process or recognise creative outcomes.

We identify a dearth of creative intelligence, thinking, skills and process.

The systems, culture and tools that have delivered us here are increasingly recognised as dysfunctional for where we wish to go. It is time for a hard reset.

Luckily we are in the perfect position.

Aristotle and his ilk were aware that the knowledge of the universe was observable within their garden, a poetic sentiment, we are living this reality with a universe of information in the palm of our hand.

In (re)discovering the necessity for creativity, should we begin to shift our values to embrace both Gold and Rouge equally, and should our goal be to cultivate wise, healthy citizens, we begin to move towards the dawn of a second Renaissance.

When information is abundant,

immediately accessible and free,

the challenge is no longer what you think... but how.

Creative skill sets, intelligence and process are not only the future, they are future proof. Imagine if every student, yourself included, could access any topic of curiosity and apply these Six Creative Skill Sets to their learning:

To research and development...

To advertising and marketing...

To storytelling, art, theatre and film...

To strategy and risk...

To data analytics and finance...

To philosophy and politics...

Creative intelligence grants you the superpower to process more diverse, dense and abstract sources of information, faster, and for more unique outcomes, than any system of A.I.

Your creative potential is limitless.

Should these values shift into focus and should this focus shift into reality, we begin to cultivate a society of Aristotles and Alexanders, of Katherine Johnsons and Frida Kahlos. Courageous, considerate, learned, compassionate, deeply curious of the world around them; a civilisation empowered by enlightened thinking, rather than dependence on tools.

3.

Collaboration

vs. Creativity

i: Inspiration

In 1937, after the bombing of Guernica, Pablo Picasso paints a portrait of his muse Dora Maar. Described as 'an amazing depiction of female grief and a metaphor for the tragedy of Spain', Picasso's Weeping Woman remains iconic within the history of modern art.

In 1974, two college dropouts conceived of a personal home computer that might fit on your dining room table. From a prototype built in a garage, the vision of Steve Jobs and Apple Computers, revolutionised business, technology and technical design, and created a legacy that surpasses his lifetime.

In 1941, Diane Nemerov eloped at 18 to marry Allan Arbus, from whom she learned photography. Influenced by documentary, fashion and photojournalistic styles, Diane Arbus shifted her focus to portray society's outcasts.
Drag queens, misfits, trailer park folk, trans, the homeless, drunk and wretched... Diane captured them all, unapologetically giving them a face and forcing us to acknowledge them

In doing so, Arbus challenged what and who we deem 'proper', 'tasteful' or 'worthy of art'. By rejecting modern media and

sensibilities, Arbus' work remains confrontational and relevant.
Quoted by Robert Hughes, Time Magazine, 1972:

'Arbus did what seemed impossible for a still photographer.
She altered our experience of the face'.

*

For most of us desiring to be creative, when we observe the
Greats, their origins and their body of work, we feel often feel
cold, dwarfed within the shadow of titans, wondering only…
'How?'

How did Picasso deconstruct human form and emotion into
geometric shapes to depict a nuanced and stark representation of
innocents exposed to war?
We don't know… but it works.

How did college drop-outs conceive and build a self-contained
home computer from spare parts, the seed of which launched
one the world's leading, innovative, digital empires?
We don't know… but it worked.

How did Arbus, using exactly the same tools as her peers, introduce the public to an entirely new and authentic experience of portraiture and the human condition?
We don't know… but it works.

Each produced a prolific body of **original** work that outlasted their respective lifetimes as legacy. Logically, none of it really makes sense and since we cannot immediately join the dots between the individual, what they produced and how they produced it, there must be only one explanation…
'They're creative'.

CREATIVITY = MAGIC
CREATIVES = SPECIAL / GENIUS

This belief has existed for a millennia.
In the time of Aristotle, it was believed to be the Muses bestowing inspiration to savants, seeding the belief that the process was wholly magical, reliant on spiritual favour.
The language that surrounds the arts is nothing short of supernatural—dancers are ethereal, actors transform, philosophers transcend, photographers may capture your soul.

Make no mistake, creatives wholly embrace these beliefs, for if creativity is esoteric and magic, then creatives are magically esoteric. To be fair, even creatives mistake much of their own process, since their work is intuitive and feels natural, and they need not dissect or translate it for others.

Jobs famously quoted...

'When you ask creative people how they did something, they feel a little guilty because they didn't really do it, they just saw something.'

Jobs also quipped...

'Creativity is just connecting things'... betraying his lack of awareness of creativity outside of his own world.

Whether dance, design or drama what you actually observe with artists is Linear Expertise aligned with high levels of **composition, emotional intelligence, adaptability** and **originality.**

Since these traits are not commonly practiced in Golden environments, they are generally bundled together to represent a single creative concept—'inspiration'.

Inspiration **solved** the **problem**.

Inspiration delivers **original** ideas.

Inspiration is the magic sauce!

One small problem, inspiration as a method is vague, not entirely manageable, reliable or scalable. Also you and I have very different ideas on what inspires us and this is part of the issue.

So when Jobs et al… create something **original** and find success, though we may be inspired by new possibilities, at the same time we also ask ourselves… 'how can I do that'?

If THEY are 'creative geniuses' and WE are not… can we ever create the way they do?

Golden logic says 'no'. Productivity insists that processes be standard and replicable. Inspiration is seldom either standard or replicable, nor is it consistent, reliable or trainable for others… another creative paradox.
Accepting this as fact, a Golden hack was invented to soothe our ego and cheat to an outcome.

Largely credited to an American, marketing executive, Alex Osborn, the term *brainstorming* was coined and popularised during the 1940's and this process was rapidly adopted as the go-to method for the inspiration of ideas.

Brainstorming offered four simple guidelines anyone could apply for free:

1. No judgement (of ideas)
2. Think freely
3. Big numbers—the more ideas the better
4. Many heads are better than one, *ie:* **collaboration**.

As a concept, brainstorming is less than 100 years old, though we find the logic and practice of collaboration thriving, globally, at every level of business and education, from primary school projects to strategy sessions on the board of multinationals. It is accepted fact that:

COLLABORATION = CREATIVITY

My question is… does it work?

Is collaboration creative?

ii: Candour

In a recent post on my LinkedIn feed, a member of the board at General Electric was lauded by the CEO of an Education Institute, it read:

• 3rd+
Board Advisory Member
1w • Edited • ⊗

"Speak up at meetings.
"What if I have nothing to say?"
"Then why attend? Just to hear? Read the minutes!"

That's one of the advice I got when I first joined Jack Welch's GE.

GE culture is about CANDOR - speaking up with frankness, disagreeing without malice.

Jack Welch explains, "When you've got candor, ...everything just operates faster and better." "Lack of candor basically blocks smart ideas, fast action, and good people contributing all the stuff they've got."

In the GE culture, you speak up because you want to contribute, not to show how smart you are.

You pushback, not to win an argument but to search for the best idea.

You listen to everyone cause the best idea can come from anyone and not just from the person with the biggest title.

When everybody has candor, the discussion is rich, decisions get made and are quickly acted on.

So before my first big meeting in GE, I went through the agenda, developed my point of view and ready to speak with candor.

That day I knew I was made for GE and GE was made for me.

When culture is strong - you don't need rules to do the right things - people just do it.

According to the author of this post...

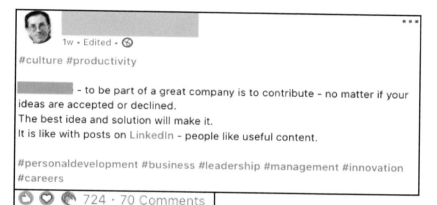

#culture #productivity

_____ - to be part of a great company is to contribute - no matter if your ideas are accepted or declined.
The best idea and solution will make it.
It is like with posts on LinkedIn - people like useful content.

#personaldevelopment #business #leadership #management #innovation #careers

724 · 70 Comments

The feedback and praise continued...

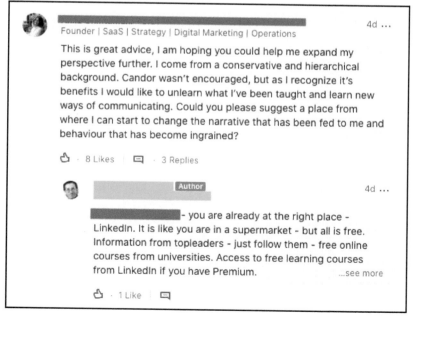

Founder | SaaS | Strategy | Digital Marketing | Operations   4d ...

This is great advice, I am hoping you could help me expand my perspective further. I come from a conservative and hierarchical background. Candor wasn't encouraged, but as I recognize it's benefits I would like to unlearn what I've been taught and learn new ways of communicating. Could you please suggest a place from where I can start to change the narrative that has been fed to me and behaviour that has become ingrained?

· 8 Likes   · 3 Replies

Author   4d ...

_____ - you are already at the right place - LinkedIn. It is like you are in a supermarket - but all is free. Information from topleaders - just follow them - free online courses from universities. Access to free learning courses from LinkedIn if you have Premium.   ...see more

· 1 Like

Observing candour in board meetings and LinkedIn discussions, we note they all abide by the four principles of brainstorming, trusting in the premise that:

Many heads + Many ideas = Best ideas and solutions

What lacks in a collaborative model is that Osborn's guidelines fail to articulate *how* an individual may think freely, or *how* you may generate a large number of ideas, or the quality/**originality** of those ideas, or to account for personality types that may best operate solo or in groups.

Collaboration is largely suited to the loudest idea in the room, is easily subverted by democracy or positions of influence, and has proven disastrous when specific expertise is necessary.

Someone with some insight may choose to raise this concern.

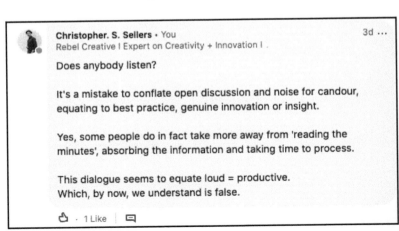

Christopher. S. Sellers • You   3d ...
Rebel Creative I Expert on Creativity + Innovation I .

Does anybody listen?

It's a mistake to conflate open discussion and noise for candour, equating to best practice, genuine innovation or insight.

Yes, some people do in fact take more away from 'reading the minutes', absorbing the information and taking time to process.

This dialogue seems to equate loud = productive.
Which, by now, we understand is false.

👍 · 1 Like   🖵

I received meagre support; one 'like' from a nice random lady, but unlike other commenters, no response at all from our Author. A post praising candour and critical thought, is met with candour and critical thought, and is ignored… we might wonder why?

*

Established as a digital platform for professionals to network, LinkedIn's demographic is predominantly formally educated, white-collar professionals who, like the author of this post, espouse their openness for candour to facilitate the free flowing marketplace of ideas.

When we review the statistics for this one post, the sentiment being collaboration = best ideas.

724 passively support this belief.
70 vocally support this belief.
1 passively critical (1 'like').
1 vocally critical (me).

In a collaborative scenario, where open candour and debate is encouraged and the best ideas rise to the top, like so much churned butter:

724 > 2

70 > 1

No doubt you've tasted this anxiety for yourself; the shudder down your spine as you realise you, and you alone, are the odd one out from your colleagues.

Within context, in a room full of peer who all agree that 'collaboration is best process', what sane individual would choose to speak up to contradict such a culture? It is much less daunting to comply with the will of the group.

Then again, some misfits do not; they must want attention, to cause a scene, they're overly negative and aren't team players.
Or perhaps they have an alternative point of view that could be of value?
How could you tell the difference?
In a collaborative environment, how would you identify high-value, atypical input?

If we return to our example, at a ratio of 70 : 1, dissent or atypical input might appear something like this:

This is a representation of how culture passively forms itself based on shared values and identity.

Perhaps our author was right to ignore X; everyone has an opinion, not all of them are valid and offering a counterpoint does not prove X to be any more correct or true.

Or perhaps X may have cut through the noise to be valued? Not the case in this example and not the case unless we 'speak up' on the G.E. Board.

Whether or not X has value is at your discretion and herein lies the issue with all of collaboration... who determines what ideas have merit?

In the case of G.E, it is Jack Welch who insists the Board speak up and employ candour, dictating the process by which ideas are developed and by extension, the value of these ideas.

Leadership dictates creative culture, process and output.

This is as true in the arts world. Directors determine the actors they cast, the roles they play and how they rehearse.

Gallery curators decide which artists they want to display and where they are featured.

Choreographers decide the routine, who gets the solo and who is in the ensemble.

Our LinkedIn author exhibits identical behaviour.

A savvy reader may note there are strategic advantages in where leadership places their attention. Responding to the lady asking for advice, our author's feedback is highlighted by the algorithm as 'valuable'. By ignoring X, the algorithm is told 'there is no value here'… dissent is masked.

Though more subtle than Jack Welch, our author's selective attention manipulates the algorithm to reframe their discussion:

'Here is my opinion. **724** professionals agree with me.

70 professionals vocally agree with us.

We're supported by the **top 10 most vocal** professionals who all agree with us'.

Examining atypical ideas, within the context of culture, do you genuinely believe... 'the best idea and solutions will make it'?

In the realm of democracy: X loses.

In the realm of leadership: X is non-compliant.

In the realm of social/organisational culture: X is not like us As.

In the realms of social media algorithms: X is of no value.

As we unstitch this narrative of collaboration and culture, we observe that, despite the rhetoric, what is prompted is neither candour nor debate—precisely the opposite.

**Culture demands compliance
and relies on echo chambers to be validated.**

**Compliance, by definition,
is the antithesis of creativity.**

iii: Echo chambers

Echo chamber: an environment in which a person encounters only beliefs or opinions that coincide with their own, so that their existing views are reinforced and alternative ideas are not considered.

'But if leaders are doing it, they must be right!'

It would be reasonable to assert that, if every organisation, cross-industry, globally, has employed brainstorming principles for the better part of a century, then they must hold some value.
Jack Welch and his Board are correct; a strong culture is conducive to social cohesion and we can achieve a lot relatively quickly when everyone is rowing in the same direction.
(Note this is a key metric of productivity).

When we observe collaboration everywhere, employed to plot strategy, improve systems, research data and design tools, perhaps we should objectively examine its efficacy as a creative process.
Let me be clear, it is not that collaboration cannot deliver ideas, it is the belief that:

- Collaboration is the **only** process to generate ideas.
- Collaboration is the **optimal** process to facilitate creativity.

And symptomatic of echo chambers...

• The rejection that there may be **any other way**.

To demonstrate what I mean, let us briefly revisit Aristotle to apply some logic and critical reasoning...

*

Collaboration believes that from multiple contributions, you will have the best of everything, therefore arrive at the best possible outcome.

A + B = C

PROBLEM + COLLABORATION = BEST IDEA

Within context of collaboration, leadership dictates process and ideas are tailored to fit the culture: the CEO may demand you speak up, an online author may insist you agree with them.

Let's imagine you have four members in a group and we simulate their input as a value.

PROBLEM + (12 + 3 + 7 + 8) = 30

Your group all agree that **30** is your best outcome, there is a 100% consensus; so what was your process and how did you arrive at this solution?

Assuming **30** is an optimal outcome, how do you validate this? Surely you would need alternative solutions and/or process to compare against—within this culture, where should you expect to find atypical thought for a comparison?

When we critically examine collaboration as process, we encounter a rather elementary discovery—collaboration more often delivers a random result, via a process of amalgamation and compromise.

PROBLEM + (A + B + C + D) = Y ?

Where organisations and online communities practise, endorse and rely on collaboration it is evident that creativity has become trapped within a Golden echo chamber.

Our LinkedIn example illustrates how these echo chambers of belief passively coalesce and that intelligence, education, status or role do not insulate you from the sweet, subtle trap of cultural compliance and cognitive bias.

2 > 724

As a result, leadership and the culture they manifests develop two dangerous, crippling blindspots:

1. **Creativity is suffocated within a culture that does not allow it to breathe.**

2. **Leadership are unable to identify creative solutions when they are offered.**

This issue of culture is precisely why so many leaders, who genuinely approach creativity in their organisation with the best of intentions, are often stifled and frustrated with the process, with so little to show for an outcome.

Even though everyone agrees with them, nothing changes, nothing improves and they don't know why, but since everyone is smart and agreed that this was 'best process'... it must be creativity's fault. Once again it has proven to be unmanageable, random and not worth the ROI.

What is particularly interesting is that while brainstorming as a model of inspiration caught popularity during the 1940s, its efficacy as a process was scientifically debunked only twenty years later.

*

In her seminal book *QUIET: The Power of Introverts in a World that Can't Stop Talking'*, Susan Cain references a study conducted by Psychology Professor, Marvin Dunnette at the University of Minnesota in 1963.

They gathered two types of test subjects: advertising executives (mostly extroverted) and engineers (mostly introverted) and recorded their ideas participating in both solitary and group, **brainstorming** sessions. The assumption was that the extroverts in advertising would thrive within group **collaboration**, where the introverts in engineering would prosper working solo. The results?

'(Both demographics)... produced more ideas when they worked on their own than when they worked as a group. They also produced ideas of equal or higher quality when working individually'.

In a report from 2000, Cain cites organisational psychologist, Adrian Furnham:

'...the evidence from science suggests that business people must be insane to use brainstorming... if you have talented, motivated people, they should be encouraged to work alone when creativity or efficiency is of the highest priority.'

*

If the goal is to allow everyone a voice, employ democratic process and engender a compliant culture:

Collaboration = Effective process

If the goal is to **solve** complex problems, **proactively innovate**, avoid **echo chambers**, **adapt** intelligently, **compose** new ideas or facilitate optimal creative thinking for specific outcomes, in an effective, productive and reliable manner.

Collaboration = Weakest process

So how can we employ a more effective creative model?
Perhaps there is another breed of professionals we could observe.

iv: The individual

Examining the belief that collaboration is the only and best practice to develop ideas, perhaps we might pause to ask... 'I wonder if anyone else has ever had a good idea?'

Should we broaden our scope to observe any body of work outside of Golden industries, we may discover something rather interesting...

Architecture: Frank Lloyd Wright, Leoh Ming Pei, Zaha Hadid.

Literature: Mary Shelley, William Shakespeare, Sappho.

Film: Quentin Tarantino, Orson Welles, Akira Kurosawa.

Cuisine: Heston Blumenthal, Julia Child, Joël Robuchon.

Photography: Helmut Newton, Nadav Kander, Diane Arbus.

Music: David Bowie, Nina Simone, Dolly Parton, Tim Minchin.

Painting: Frida Kahlo, Pablo Picasso, Jackson Pollock, Banksy.

Philosophy: Confucius, Simone de Beauvoir, Aristotle.

Every name is an example of Applied Creativity personified: they harmonise their Linear Expertise with Creative Intelligence to produce a prolific body of work as leaders in their field.

You may note they all share one common anomaly: they are all individuals. But this is different right? These are the exceptional exceptions, rather than the rules, our immediate reflex is to declare…

I can't dance, paint, sing, cook or design a house… I can't do what artists do!

Remember that cooking, painting, dancing and singing involve their own Linear Expertise; each has their own requirements, knowledge and skill that one must learn in order to be competent. You can learn these skills—singing is more an understanding of how to project vowel sounds than it is gifted talent.

A chef must understand julienne, chiffonade, brunoise and mincing to demonstrate competent knife technique—knowledge you could learn in five minutes—a skill you would spend a lifetime perfecting.

If you only observe the outcome—the stark **originality** of Picasso's Weeping Woman, Nina Simone's raw **emotional** power and range—you dismiss the skill, intelligence, discipline and craft each of these artistic practices demand.

It is the Magic Trick Paradox; you marvel at the illusion, because the craft is expertly hidden.

We infer the same bias toward **C7** as the only survivor of the Hotel Room; we observe an exceptional individual who achieved something incredible, on their own, despite all the odds, when no-one else could. It is a convenient, attractive and powerful narrative that robs you of your creative authority.

CREATIVITY = MAGIC
CREATIVES = SPECIAL / GENIUS

Instead of 'special' perhaps you recognise how each individual demonstrates mastery of their Linear Expertise.

Instead of 'magic' perhaps you identify traits like **adaptability, innovation, emotional intelligence** and how they're applied to **solve** complex issues or **compose** something **original**.

Gradually the clouds of mystique shrouding creativity begin to evaporate...

CREATIVITY ≠ MAGIC
CREATIVES ≠ SPECIAL/GENIUS

Individuals employing Creative Skill Sets may produce extraordinary results.

If we dare to strip away the professional facade and are honest with ourselves, there is a simple explanation why collaboration has become so popular and so fervently defended.
It is comfortable and it is easy.

There is safety in numbers; if we fail, we fail together, my ego (and career) is preserved. Corporate culture treats this as professional practice and in order to insulate themselves from embarrassment, leadership elect to outsource many of their projects to third-parties. As a result, there is limited creative development, limited maturation of creative process, limited accountability and zero retention of creative intelligence.

Creatively speaking, in Golden cultures, there seems to be an unspoken, terrifying fear of standing up, being seen, being heard and being accountable; traits intrinsic to creative process, traits good leadership should exemplify.

By comparison, we observe a very different ethic demonstrated by the artists on our list:

'It is my project, my voice, my process, my work and I am accountable.'

Much like writing this book and tipping over this particular apple cart, I am aware this may make many uncomfortable and like my comment on LinkedIn, my purpose is not to be a misfit for fun, rather to challenge the thinking and process that accepts collaboration as undeniably true.

If you genuinely believe collaboration is effective, it must be asked...

Personally or professionally...
what alternative creative process do you have?

What creative intelligence do you possess,
that does not rely on the input of others?

*

Additionally:

- Do you believe for every challenge, project and relationship, you will always have savvy, intelligent colleagues around you?

- What happens when your team isn't available, are you suddenly less creative?

- If you outsource the responsibility to others, how do you critically evaluate creative solutions offered to you?

These are some of the questions you should ask if you wish to assess the validity and efficacy of creative process within your organisation.

Therefore, when creative process cannot be engendered via compliance—and optimal practice may not be found within the collective—there is only one logical outcome.

Optimal creativity will come from you... X ... the individual.

v: Prolific. Proactive. Leading. Original.

There is one last powerful distinction between the culture of
collaboration versus the individual.

Picasso did more than paint one woman, once.

A sculptor, printmaker, ceramist and stage designer, Picasso was
influenced by a myriad of styles and produced a prolific body of
work before inventing cubism, an entirely new artistic movement.
A career and style that evolved over decades, Picasso dynamically
influenced theory, practice and standards to revolutionise the art
world, an impact which continues long after his death.

Prolific. Proactive. Leading. Original.

We can observe the moral of Picasso in Steve Jobs, Diane Arbus,
Shakespeare and Aristotle.

Prolific. Proactive. Leading. Original.

Nikolai Tesla, Stephen Sondheim, Nina Simone, Friedrich
Nietzsche, Yayoi Kusama.

Prolific. Proactive. Leading. Original.

Fridha Kahlo, Leonardo Da Vinci, Shunpei Yamazaki, Brett
Whiteley, Bob Dylan.

Prolific. Proactive. Leading. Original.

This behaviour is consistent historically, globally, and cross-industry, demonstrating that the creative potency and productivity of the individual eclipses any comparable attempt of a collective.

This may initially feel daunting, as though we are comparing ourselves to giants. Whenever we begin to learn a new language and compare ourselves to those who are fluent, we feel overwhelmed as amateurs, as if WE will never be as good as THEM.

Two things... first, remember that one half of this equation is your Linear Expertise, which you already have. Whatever your profession, passion or past-time, you've gained valuable knowledge, skills and experience; these are not to be dismissed, rather they are enhanced by your creativity.

Second, as individuals, these artists, craftsmen, innovators and thinkers revolutionised their respective industries by learning what was available, challenging what was accepted and creating something new.

The equation for creativity is two-fold:

1. **Individually we must develop our own creative skills and intelligence.**

2. **Creative Intelligence must be recognisable to peers/leadership.**

Again, this is a challenge of language and translation; no matter your individual fluency, should your creative ideas fall on deaf ears, no conversation can be had.

Unfortunately, this is a conflict that both the professional and the amateur will have to brace for throughout the entirety of their careers.

*

Of Picasso's first cubist attempt, 'Les Demoiselles d'Avignon'—a representation of five naked women—one of Pablo's closest friends, Georges Braque, remarked:

> 'To paint in such a way was as bad as drinking petrol in the hope of spitting fire.'

A friend and fellow artist didn't even 'get' Picasso.

That prototype Jobs and Wozniak built in their garage, was pulled together from spare Atari parts and they approached Atari in the hopes of exchanging their proof of concept for roles in the company. Atari rejected them outright.

They tried again with programming giant Hewlett-Packard, only to be told:

'...we don't need you. You haven't gone through college yet.'

The value of creative ideas are dictated by leadership and their culture.

A photographer of freaks, Arbus' images were raw and confronting and for this very reason, drew criticism from contemporary photographer, Susan Sontag, who declared:

'Arbus's village houses only idiots. I might call her art instead an inspired autism.'

Even other creatives may be challenged by those who distort a purists medium.

So what should we do... should we not try?

If creative resistance is all around us (and within us) should we give in, give up, give it all away?

Is creativity really the domain of the delusional, the defiant the unhinged, the unrelenting, the gifted and the lucky?

To survive an unreceptive environment…

To endure and thrive in spite of it…

Is not a story exclusive to creativity or creatives.

Criticism, discomfort, confusion and rejection are conditions of life, not exclusive to creativity or creatives—you could taste all four on a bad date.

To face these challenges demands a level of **emotional** maturity, confidence in your ability, humility in your flaws and the conviction to remain strong when bracing the **risk** of the unknown.

Perhaps it is not creativity that makes you brave and bold.

Perhaps you must be brave to be boldly creative.

4.

Emotions

+ Risk

i: I can't draw...

One year for my birthday, a friend invited me to a life drawing class.
Though I don't consider myself able to draw, I figured... 'I'm creative'... and it would be fun to try something different.

Downstairs in a small performance space of a local bar, an intimate crowd of amateur artists set up with pencils, charcoal, paper and wine: our live model took position as a respectful audience began to sketch.
Pencil in hand, sober with my limitations, I began to sketch, confident and eager to play. Within minutes the reality of what was on the page was punching me in the face...

'This is shit.'

I flip the page. Start fresh.
A few more minutes of poses and sketches. It's not any better. It's probably worse.
A quick scan around the room and everyone appears serene, illustrating with grace. I feel hot. It's shame. I want to cry.
I check the time. it's been seven minutes, the session is two hours. I want to escape.

This makes no sense. I know I'm creative, I know I'm good at other things. I understand drawing is not one of them. I'm an adult... why is it affecting me like this? Internally I'm screaming: 'I'm not a failure'!

Going into the evening, I believed I could not draw. By the end of the evening I **knew** I could not draw.

*

In my thirties, I decided to learn how to tap dance. Despite no background in dance, I figured I'm reasonably co-ordinated so I didn't anticipate too many challenges.

Arriving with fresh shiny tap shoes at my first beginners class, I note I'm the only boy in the room (something you get used to within the arts). Nevertheless, I take my place in front of the mirror as the instructor cues the music and counts us in...
    '5... 6... 7... 8...'

It was utterly overwhelming. Everything moved too fast. Everyone seemed to know each other. It was humiliating to be dwarfed by an ensemble of women all rapidly stamping in time.
    'What's the point? I can't follow the steps, this is stupid'!

After a loud, sweaty, ninety-minute session, embarrassed, ashamed and emasculated, I'd learned exactly nothing, other than 'I can't dance.'

*

I've always had an affinity with the French and took it upon myself to learn the language.
I began by teaching myself, studying phrasebooks, sitting in French cafés and flirting with waitresses. Mastering the basics of conversation and with dreams of living in Europe, I sought to polish my literacy and enrolled in formal French classes

I breezed through the first few semesters where games, rhymes and conversation were common, until we graduated to the more technical syllabus of grammar—immediately my learning fell off a cliff.
Every evening I begged the tutor to put the sentence in context:

'Mademoiselle, s'il vous plait… Francois et Louise, took the bus to WHERE? WHEN?'
'Oh Christophe… subject plus verb, plus past-participle est les destination'.

I quit French classes.

Three experiences you can probably relate to.

If nothing else, hopefully this book demonstrates that drawing, languages and dancing are skills that can be learned, not a core lack of talent or failure of personality, and if you cannot tap, perhaps hip hop or ballet is more your jam.

However, to learn this Linear Expertise, we are utterly at the mercy of our peers and for every executive I've coached, to every child I've tutored, one phrase haunts me as the most tragic:

"I'm not creative."

It's always a casual, throw-away line, like commenting on the weather. What's sadder, is that this sentiment is always attached to an identical backstory:

' I had a… **[teacher/parent]** … who said I couldn't **[skill]**'.

Joking about my life drawing experience to my mother, she remarked:

'You used to love to draw, until Mr Butler threw your picture in the bin.'

A primary school teacher, rejecting the portrait I'd drawn of him, was enough to quash my desire to ever draw again. I was eight years old.

It's in the formative stage of our youth that we are exposed to many new and strange hobbies; this is a time when Rouge is our intuitive language for connection, understanding and expression. To be rejected, judged, mocked (or worse, ignored) impacts us on deep, emotional and psychological levels which are not readily understood.

If we've difficulty deciphering foreign grammar, we are stupid and cannot speak languages.

If we cannot master dance steps with the class, it's because we're uncoordinated and clumsy.

If we cannot sketch nudes, it's because we're untalented and not creative.

These feelings of shame, of being diminished, are often so potent and deeply rooted that they may deter us from ever trying again. It is natural to censor these feelings and avoid the risk of failure, to preserve our ego and spare ourselves pain.

This brings us to the core of why we avoid our own creativity and why we are generally apprehensive toward creative process—people are believed to be **risk**-averse. This explanation is quick and easy, and like most hacks, rather superficial.

In business, **risk** is a commercial assessment; **risk**-aversion seems logical so as not to waste resources. However, this **risk** rationale makes less sense when applied to everyday hobbies.

Why are we so terrified of public speaking?
Why don't we pursue our passions to draw or dance or learn a new language?
And why can't we commit to these pursuits during our initial ugly duckling phase?

Because would-be experts omit two deeply rooted human conditions that make genuine change possible.

1. Risk

2. Emotion

These two dynamics are inextricably linked to the core of your creative potential and, regardless of Linear competency, unless you address the root cause, your potential will forever be limited. Let's deal with **risk** first.

ii: Risk

As a species we are genetically wired and socially engineered to avoid **risk.** The unknown berries could be poisonous, the strangers could be a threat, the world's most common phobia of public speaking is less a literal fear of talking to groups of people, than it is a primal instinct to be wary of many pairs of eyes focused on you.

What is fascinating is how immediate our **risk** response is, how broadly it manifests and how imperceptible it is and how rigidly it establishes itself.

To illustrate this trigger-happy fail-safe, over the page is a creative exercise I've designed to flex your risk response.

*

In thirty seconds complete this sequence.

Sketch your solution below or on a piece of paper:

A ———————— **B** ———————— ..... ———————— .....

For most, the immediate answer is:

Congratulations, you are correct, however, there may be alternative solutions to this puzzle.

It is equally logical that the series repeats or mirrors itself.

A ——————— B ——————— A ——————— B

A ——————— B ——————— B ——————— A

There is also…

A ——————— B ——————— 1 ——————— 2

A ——————— B ——————— ∀ ——————— B

A ——————— B ——————— α ——————— β

I use to this exercise to demonstrate the principle of **risk.**
This is a puzzle with no predetermined outcome; there are
dozens of potential solutions you could create, all of which
would be correct, supported by their own logic.

In Rouge we term these as creative choices.
The goal is to work through all the 'safe' and 'easy' choices to
find the bold, strong and dynamic creative choices.
It's a fun little exercise that yields some interesting insights...
watch what happens when we give it a twist and apply some
context to this exercise.

*

Imagine that this puzzle represents the need for a new strategy or
a solution to a problem.

You will be assigned a $100,000 budget to invest in **one** solution.
You can only choose one and you must explain your rationale.
This where things start to get interesting...

Cognitively, you recognise all of your solutions are logical, correct, effective and equivalent.

However, the more your solutions deviate from the norm (**A, B, C, D**)... the more **risk** it **feels** you create.

You start to feel uneasy, unsure, you doubt, you wonder if other people will 'get it'.

With a $100,000 budget on the line, including your career, reputation and ego, why go for something abstract?

It makes more sense to 'reduce friction', make the safe choice, and secure the deal with something you know your audience will go for.

Therefor, by calculation of **risk**, you are more likely to:

Prefer A, B, C, D since you recognise it and it **feels** safe.
Provide A, B, C, D since it is more likely to be accepted.

A small, insidious detail, it's subtle, but it's there and here is why you should be concerned.

We've examined how education provides standardised Linear process and we understand how the collective will influence what the 'best input' will be.

When both environments are highly **risk-avoidant**, intelligence becomes reframed:

RECOGNISABLE = OPTIMAL SOLUTION

(rather than…)

CREATIVE ≈ OPTIMAL SOLUTION

Within this schema is the unconscious bias that all important decisions, solutions and outcomes must be recognisable in order to be valid, safe, and correct.

It's not that our **risk** response is wrong, more that it is immature and underdeveloped since our **emotional** need to feel safe conflicts and overrides our cognitive intelligence.

As a self-aware species, we understand **risk**, our avoidant nature and the need to overcome it to attain reward: this dynamic is usually discussed theoretically without much consideration for context. For corporate, **risk** is examined purely as a financial equation: profit vs loss, capital vs ROI.

In reality, **risk** is an **emotionally intelligent** assessment, rooted within each of us individually and exists as a personal and tangible concern.

*

There is the story of the 'loneliest whale' whose unique mating call resonates at 52-hertz.
Unique in that no other whale shares this frequency.
Unique also, that 52-hertz is too high a frequency to be heard by other whales.
We, as humans, can hear him—we objectively identify his uniqueness—but to his own kind he appears not to exist, singing out to the deep, dark in a language that no-one understands.
So he roams the oceans calling out for companionship, unaware that his world is deaf.
Our whale paints a powerful moral until you realise, male humans have a their own distinct mating calls.

The Gold standard for male ambition, intelligence and success is oft equated to material accoutrements, offering the promise of stability, safety and security. Personally speaking, as a male who has never aspired to the nine-to-five, car-career-home-suit package, this paints me in a rather obtuse light to any potential female partner.

The ability to tap dance, speak French, draw nudes or write books, obscures the Warrior-Provider archetype. Whales or humans, to be unrecognisable to a potential mate is a primal, potent and genuine **risk**.

The reward for being unique is originality.
The risk of being unique is singularity.

Luckily, not all humans are whales, so one has the option to **adapt**, put on a tie and fit in. Or maintain the ideal that there is **original** value in X within an ocean of As.

*

Understanding that risk is a genetically encoded reflex, there is no shame in gravitating towards what is known and recognisable, whether it be personal or professional practice.

However, without critical examination, everything not immediately identifiable becomes perceived as a **risk**, and simultaneously misleads us to believe that only that which we immediately recognise can be good, safe, correct and true.

Within a **risk-averse** mindset you can never lead, only follow, mimic and recite as you continue to churn out weak creative choices:

Problem-solving is formulaic and demands a framework.

Innovation is permitted in 1% increments to 'play it safe'.

Composition regurgitates over-used themes.

Adaptability is handicapped.

Emotional Intelligence atrophies.

Originality is dismissed as impossible or 'just a remix'.

All of this contributes to a slow, exhausting, expensive, inefficient and ineffective process, until suddenly, someone offers something new, a quantum leap that changes the game and how you play, prompting a collective, exasperated sigh of...

'Why didn't we see this before?'

In pursuing creativity and its related skill sets, we would be wise to critically evaluate **risk** in order to distil it from primal fears, personal insecurities or professional bias and to summon the courage to challenge it where necessary. To do this we must face **risk**, step into the unknown and wade through the murky, turgid waters of uncomfortable **emotions**.

iii: Emotions

There is one particular difference that startles me whenever I work with Golden clients and that is the complete desensitisation of the individual from their work.

No-one feels... anything.

It's the classic 'leave your problems at the door'... an odd sentiment considering your average employee will often spend more of their life within the workplace, than with those they love. When we examine the cost of **emotionally** detached work, we find:

- Career burnout.
- Corrosive effects on mental health.
- Alcohol and substance abuse.
- Relationship breakdowns.

That these issues are systemic and non-specific to age/sex/role, it is no surprise we observe a demand for **E.Q** in the workplace. Soft/communication skills, empathy in leadership, resilience in teams, work/life balance, even the sentiment of 'connecting to your passion' is to ensure a longer career lifespan and greater productivity.

Pandemics cast a spotlight on this issue by disrupting the standard work model and, by default, proving that productivity is achievable in a non-standard format.

In fact, current practice has compounded the need for **emotional intelligence** as individuals and organisations are respectively forced to become more flexible in managing atypical work practice and cultivate healthy, sustainable cultures. Still, our notion of work remains the same...

WORK = cognitive / mechanical function

(How you feel is irrelevant)

*

The arts, by contrast, are perhaps the polar opposite... everyone feels EVERYTHING!

Ask an artist about their process and they'll reply, 'I just felt...' and describe their work in analogies.

You have a hard time attracting artists to a project if they are not intrinsically motivated to its cause.

Artists also retain the luxury of choosing to work with people they like and ignoring those they don't.

When we compare the ethic and output artists apply to their work:

- Artists are **proactive** in their craft.
- Invest greater personal time and resources to projects.
- Are self-disciplined to independently train/rehearse/create.
- Produce at a consistently high standard.

When you consider much of an artist's work is often achieved independently, without supervision, the results are nothing short of phenomenal. In fact, if Golden industries could capture a fraction of an artist's work ethic, it would shatter their expectations of what productivity is.

So, if your goal is reliable, high-quality output, within a healthy, sustainable culture, you may ask—what separates a Rouge/artistic workplace from a Golden/corporate workplace?
For all the superfluous differences, one ethic divides the two:

In the arts, your emotions have value.

What underpins healthy organisational cultures, specifically creative cultures where one is encouraged to explore **risk**, is the need to feel safe—this is a purely emotional need.

Not psychological.

'Psychological safety' to build trust is another Golden mistranslation; this definition relies on external conditions (similar to collaboration) to provide comfort, support and space for teams to be productive, reinforcing the belief that your individual, personal **emotions** are irrelevant in a professional setting.

*

It is high-minded to believe that our **emotions** have no place in business.

I've always appreciated the story of young Ferruccio, an Italian tractor mechanic, who mentioned to Enzo Ferrari that his latest model suffered from a weak clutch and suggested a tractor clutch would prevent them from breaking.
When Enzo laughed in his face, insulting and dismissing the youngster, the next year Ferruccio started building his own sports cars. Lamborghini was born out of spite.

Revenge, frustration, envy and greed, motivate and inspire us, as much as altruism, charity or love.

Our **emotions** are a potent resource; they inform, protect, inspire and when wielded judiciously, ignite unlimited potential.
To deny their relevance not only diminishes your capacity, but generates its own detrimental side-effects.

Much of my early work in L&D was designing role-play scenarios for medical graduates. Years of intensive training had taught them to view a patient objectively; a body was a machine with moving parts, a useful technique to improve diagnostic and surgical competency.
However, the same technique, routinely practised, had served to amputate empathy from these graduates; a less positive trait when it came to bedside manner or negotiating with next of kin.
From a cursory observation of burnout, substance abuse and suicide rates amongst medical professionals, you realise that it is not only their patients at **risk**.

So why do we avoid, relegate and dismiss our emotions?
There's a few reasons—a deeply engrained culture of productivity has a lot to answer for though the disconnect more wholly lies in the belief that emotions are random, unproductive and unmanageable... another Golden myth.

What is true, is that **emotional** skills are rarely addressed within a standard format. Schooling and employment are **emotionally** inert environments and it is left to the random hand of 'nurture' or social conditioning to develop them as a means of survival. Left to our own devices, in our own environment, this has serious drawbacks. Socially, the ethos of 'boys don't cry' has proven to be utterly destructive in the **emotional** development of men. In turn, women are 'hysterical' or 'bitches' if they choose to share their **emotions** or assert their influence.

Professionally, HR initiatives to foster a 'safe space' in organisations rarely facilitate the genuine article. Genuine trust is established when individuals feel safe in positions of vulnerability; this entails all of the **emotions** on the spectrum, not just the sanitised versions we present to our colleagues.

This is where the arts eclipses all others in the realms of practical **emotional intelligence**.
Artistic practice is the only medium by which one may **proactively** develop **emotional intelligence** by routinely challenging you to consider multiple **emotional** points of view. Where medical graduates train for Linear competency and **emotional** detachment… Artists train for Linear competency with **emotional** connection.

iv: The Arts

Imagine a space where you're allowed to swear out loud with no repercussions. A space where you had permission to hate someone and to tell them exactly why they've pissed you off. Where you could confess your most embarrassing crush and all the things you long to do with them.

A space where you could make bad jokes, fail, laugh, share, cry, be confused, doubt, fight, lose and win... then move on and you are still accepted as a valid and worthy human.

Fucking awesome.

If this sounds like a ridiculous, cathartic, fantasy land, you might be right: this is your standard rehearsal room.

The environment required to take **emotional risks**, to be vulnerable, and in doing so, trust that you will still be ok on the other side, is the core of healthy individuals, relationships and workplace cultures. The corporate term 'safe space' was adopted from theatre ensembles. For fun, let's step into an audition to demonstrate how this is practiced.

*

One October morning, I quietly caught the train to Sydney for my final audition for acting college. I'd passed the entrance audition a few weeks earlier (I hadn't told anyone) and for this final round was to perform three pieces, solo, to a panel of four directors.

Standard requirements for an acting audition:

- One classic monologue (usually a Shakespeare).
- One contemporary monologue (anything you like).
- Perhaps a song to demonstrate vocal range.

For my contemporary, I chose a monologue from *Europe* by Michael Gow—the break-up between Barbara; a European actress, and me, Douglas: a younger Australian who'd pursued her to Europe.

For weeks I had rehearsed in secret, and now I finally had the chance to unleash my soul! After a powerful rendition of angst, where I'm left defiant, confused heart-broken and alone, I was offered a polite round of applause from the panel, until asked by one of the directors…

'That was great! Could you try it as if you're on an infomercial, selling a bargain'?

In any other industry, this is a ludicrous request.

For an actor, **emotional** flexibility is a key skill set for the job.

Could I, on command, **adapt**, shifting from a heartbroken, lost boy, to self-assured con-man?

To be **emotionally** rigid would be extremely limiting in the types of roles I could play (Romeo is chalk to Richard III's cheese).

This test, like assessing skills competency in an interview, would demonstrate how **emotionally** flexible I was and indicate how much of a challenge I may be to train over the next three years. (I passed the audition and was accepted to college—I was no less difficult to train).

Similar techniques are employed in every artistic field, designed to assess, challenge and stretch ones **emotional** range. In doing so, artistic training fosters a rigorous discipline of **emotional** introspection.

If a scene requires **[emotion]**...
Where do these feelings come from...?
How does this manifest in me...?
Why I do behave like this...?
Why do I feel like this...?

The supplementary talent to this discipline is that you develop the resources to recognise, distil and process your **emotions**.

While feelings of lust, doubt, jealousy and rage may consume us at times, you learn that each is natural and, despite our initial discomfort, they are entirely manageable.

As an artist, the job is to summon these **emotions** on command, then step out of character, walk off stage and function as a 'normal' human being.
This **emotional** development as a critical and valued skill set, is what defines the arts as exemplars of practical **emotional intelligence**.

Objectively understanding, feeling and processing **emotions**, allows you to sing, shape, paint, sculpt, draw and speak with depth, clarity and authenticity. Uncomfortable **emotions** need not be feared, suppressed, dismissed or avoided, since they are not a threat to us—they are not a **risk.**

Seldom in other industries do you explore multiple ways to process information.

Only in the arts do you explore multiple ways to process emotions.

Now, here's the ugly truth that neither side confesses to...
This process is gross.

Emotional development is not all inspired learnings from battles hard won; shining a light into the darker corners of the room illuminates all the trash you threw out of sight.
Betrayal. Loss. Childhood trauma. Insecurities. Longing.
Unresolved questions. Shame. The want to make your parents proud. The resentment that that's still a desire.
We all have them, these are just a few of mine.

Emotional growth is uncomfortable and challenging; we flinch at the unsavoury elements of our personality, we're ashamed of our insecurities; to unpack and reason with them often feels exhausting and confusing.
None of this is pleasant. Neither is it quick. And here is where **risk** re-emerges—like a snake swallowing its own tail—attempting to keep you safe.

This **emotional** discomfort is translated by an immature **risk** response as 'I'm in danger'. You've either been here before and experienced pain or you've not been here before and don't recognise it.

This pattern of **risk-aversion** plays out to a familiar dead end:

TRUST

VULNERABILITY

RISK

AVOIDANCE

This pattern of **risk-avoidance** is as accurate for the individual as it is for the conglomerate. To **risk** this discomfort is no small feat; for each of us, these **emotions** are visceral and real.

However, when you develop the objectivity to distil your sense of discomfort from what is a 'threat', you expose your insecurities to the warm light of reason and, in doing so, cultivate a more informed, mature **risk** response.

Emotionally intelligent **risk** plays out in a much more beneficial, healthier, sustainable cycle.

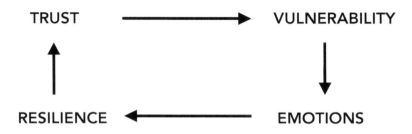

You begin to broaden your **emotional** capacity, your thinking and, in turn, your world view.

What was previously impossible, now feels achievable, because you've survived 'impossible' before.

People's motivations feel less abrasive since you recognise similar behaviour of your own; this fosters deeper empathy and a more centred self-assured nature—two highly valuable traits in leadership.

Strange ideas spark curiosity rather than apprehension; they're no longer a threat to your security.

You've a desire to learn and explore, at the very least you know that trying won't kill you, it's not that much of a **risk**.

Mature **emotional** intelligence provides you the intrinsic platform of trust to take these **risks**; it is an innate, personal resource, developed within oneself—not a comfort blanket bestowed by others.

The question only you can answer is, is it worthwhile?

Are you willing to **risk** the reward?

*

At about this time I usually meet someone declaring:

'I'm not an Artist… I work in **[insert field]**…how are **emotions** relevant'?

A trait of intelligence linked to creativity is cognitive flexibility, the ability to observe information through a myriad of lenses. What Rouge students apply, that Golden students omit, is an **emotional** lens to their medium.

Often this is intuitive, artists tend to roll with 'what feels right'. Sometimes it is by design. Sometimes it is both.

The analogy of Gold + Rouge helps simplify a complex idea to discuss it with more ease and it feels right to me.

Herein lies the dormant superpower of **emotional intelligence**:

ABSTRACT INTELLIGENCE

Artists employ **Abstract Intelligence** to articulate complex thoughts, feelings and ideas.

Music is an abstract language: dots and lines equate to notes we can play and sounds we hear.

Sculpture, painting, photography, all employ shape, light, tone, contrast, texture, dimension and shade to tell their stories.

Writers employ analogy and metaphor as abstract methods of conveying **emotional** insight. 'Mind's eye'… 'sweet sorrow'… neither are literal descriptions, Shakespeare offers these concepts to provide clarity into a characters inner-world.

What is sexy is that you, the audience, intuitively understand this language. You may not be knowledgeable in symbolism or metaphor, but you intuitively understand that broad, black strokes on a canvas, represent darker themes of death, depression and chaos.

How the sound of deep, sustained bass notes, in music, represents the same…

How dark, heavy contrast of shadowed figures in a photograph, represents the same…

How a dancer slumped, dragging their feet in slow, heavy tread, represents the same…

How is it that you understand all of these themes—this abstract conversation—when there is no literal translation or data point—and you've likely never been taught 'how to' before?
You feel it.

If you can recognise the language, you can learn the language.

A most valuable benefit of **Abstract Intelligence** is that when applied to processing information, it is infinitely scalable to complex conditions, where Linear Expertise hits a wall.
When information is representative, rather than purely Linear/literal, it offers exponentially more value, flexibility, solutions, imagination, possibilities and creative potential.

Algebra demonstrates the principle of **Abstract Intelligence** (without the **emotional** demand):

$$A + B + C + D = 30$$

- The values are representative.
- The conditions are not fixed.
- There are multiple potential solutions.

If you can learn algebra (and most of us had to) you've already taken a step in proving these creative skills may be taught, measured, developed and practically applied.

Suppressing your **emotional** resources not only handicaps empathy and ethical decision-making, you censor your potential to interpret information in **abstract** methods. In turn, you inhibit your ability to **solve**, **adapt**, **innovate**, **compose** or find anything **original**.

v: Failure

Risk and reward are the forces that propel your creative journey, though often produce an unsavoury by-product we cannot ignore. Failure.

To tell a joke and no-one laughs.

The hot, new café that faded with a whimper

Know what's worse than performing to an empty theatre?

Performing a one-man show to an audience of two... I know... I've done it...It was brutal.

Failure is a common, observable outcome of many new endeavours and, unfortunately, this subliminal correlation is all-too-familiar packaging for creative pursuits:

NEW	**=**	**RISK**	**=**	**FAILURE**
(different)		(unease)		(expected)

Any entrepreneur, any founder, any artist, will share a common narrative of hustle, struggle, mockery, rejection, silence.... until finally... a breakthrough.

If you are ever to embark on your own creative journey, whether it's an artistic passion, like Picasso or a new venture, like the two Steves, where shall you develop the **emotional** resilience to endure the ridicule, rejection and rebuke?

Where shall you develop the patience and conviction to sustain yourself during the months you suck?

If you find you are the only X, how should you gather the resolve to challenge a world of As ?

There is a popular corporate philosophy of 'make failure your friend'… seek it out… embrace it… use it as fuel!

I find this sentiment to be as immature as a **risk-avoidant** philosophy.

The blind adoration of **risk** and ethos of rewarding high-risk strategy was a culture that orchestrated the implosion of Enron and the like in the early 2000s: a corporate meltdown that could have been avoided and saved billions, had they listened to legitimate concerns.

Unlike Alice in Wonderland, perhaps we should not drink all and eat all that is put in front of us.

While the narrative of failure reads as iterative and necessary during the journey to success, these setbacks are often the observations of hindsight and should not be conflated as 'green lights' on a roadmap to greatness!

No-one sets out to fail, nor should you.

Blind risk-encouragement is as immature as risk-avoidance and I'd offer that there is a sober, **emotionally intelligent** approach to risk that equally withstands Golden critical analysis.

So how might you do this?

How can you flex your **risk** response to develop your own **emotional intelligence**?

Where Linear teaching provides a standardised process for standardised outcomes, to flex your creativity it is beneficial to explore exercises with **no predetermined outcome**.

Conveniently, the arts fit this brief nicely, offering a kaleidoscope of options that facilitate the creative concept of **play**:

PLAY = Exploration without attachment to outcome.

Play is a critical component of creative process and is often misconstrued in Golden evaluation, since **play** does not deliver an immediate, measurable or tangible product.

We observe **play** in musicians 'jamming'.

We see illustrators **play**, doodling on a pad.

Philosophy invites you to **play** with notions of truth, morality and success, leading you to explore what it might mean to be a worthwhile human; in doing so, develop your own **emotional** resilience and wisdom, a journey Socrates would applaud.

If we genuinely wish to cultivate healthier sustainable cultures, perhaps there is some wisdom in Nietzsche's advocacy for suffering or Epicurus' four rules for satisfaction.

Playing with music (via any instrument) or with colour theory (via any medium) encourages **emotional** expression, develops **composition**, and hones your **Abstract Intelligence**.

Dancing will get you fit, develop your co-ordination and balance and facilitate **emotional** release. **Playing** with choreography, timing, rhythm and tempo develops **composition** and **adaptability**.

Playing in an acting class trains public speaking and presentation skills. Improvisation, specifically, develops your ability to **adapt, innovate** and **compose original** concepts in real time.

Within your industry, it may be as simple as asking;
'What hasn't been done before…?' to prompt an exploration of ideas, systems and process. You may begin to look outside your sphere to **play** with different ideas on how you might **innovate** and **problem-solve.**

Giving yourself permission to **play**, to explore a hobby, medium or idea, without attachment to an outcome, alleviates your sense of **risk** and the fear of failure that so commonly dissuades us. In turn, you broaden your curiosity and confidence to taste new things… salty, sweet, bitter or smooth… not everything will be to your palate, but trying won't kill you.

*

Despite failing in tap class, I believed that maybe there was another way to learn.

Swallowing my pride, I approached the instructor after the class to ask if they could walk me through the routine, beat by beat, so I could match the technical steps with the tempo of the music. I was sure that if I could actually see their feet, step by step, I would be fine—I would **play** with the steps, at home, on my own.

Within two weeks I'd mastered the routine and was performing double pick-ups during my solo.

*

Dictation of grammar was eroding my confidence and love for the French language and since this tutor was unable to **adapt**... I had to.

I changed the language settings on my phone, emails and web browsers to French.

I found that playing video games in French was more immersive than watching movies with subtitles, as it challenged me to translate on my own and I practised my literacy when writing in my journals.

I'm not fluent, barely conversational, but I managed to preserve my love for the language.

I wasn't stupid: the style of teaching wasn't conducive to how I learn, so I needed to **adapt**.

I found a way to **play** with the language to help me learn.

*

I still can't draw, but it's a skill I could develop.

I'm not untalented or lack creativity, I had a prick of a teacher once... looking at you, Mr Butler.

I'm currently teaching myself sleight of hand card magic and planning to learn the banjo.

Voudrais-tu voir un tour de cartes?

5.

Six Creative

Skill Sets

Welcome to Rouge 101

What follows is a breakdown of the Six Creative Skill Sets, the building blocks of creativity and your introduction to Rouge as a language. I'm going to review each skill objectively, define their role and demonstrate how each behaves independently.

Before we start, remember that for each example, every industry requires its own Linear Expertise. Mechanics must learn to understand engines... doctors, human biology... actors, learn dialogue and how not to walk into props on stage.

As discussed, we tend to find skills like **problem-solving** and **innovation** more observable in corporate fields, while **emotional intelligence** and **originality** seem more observable in the arts. I say 'observable', not 'inherent to', a common mistranslation by both Gold and Rouge.

By examining each trait individually, I'll demonstrate that developing your creative thinking, skills and process is much more manageable when you clearly understand what is involved —that you are far more creatively competent than you first thought and that creative fluency is absolutely within reach.

1. Problem-solving

2. Innovation

3. Composition

4. Adaptability

5. Emotional Intelligence

6. Originality

Problem-solving

Fix what's broken / Overcome a challenge

(reactive)

1. Problem-solving: (reactive)

Fix what's broken/Overcome a challenge

Problem-solving is first, as the most common Creative Skill Set. **Problem-solving** is fundamentally **reactive**: a **problem** must exist in order for you to **solve** it, a challenge must emerge for you to overcome it.

Mechanics **problem-solve** on a daily basis: 'My car won't start, it makes a funny sound but won't turn over'. From this cursory information, a skilled mechanic may narrow down a diagnosis, similarly to a doctor consulting a patient—a few questions, a peek under the hood and each may efficiently treat your issue.

Effective **problem-solving** commonly relies on Linear expertise. The more knowledge and experience your mechanic has with engines, the more quickly and effectively they may solve your problem.

Sudoku and crosswords are **problem-solving** games; you require basic numeracy/literacy to play, working with incomplete information, to recognise patterns, decipher clues and find the one correct solution.

As a creative skill, **problem-solving** will always be in demand to 'fix what's broken' and is critical in overcoming personal and professional challenges in life

Meeting obstacles is commonly where your **problem-solving** skills are flexed and in a professional capacity, your Linear expertise is often sufficient.

However, life is known to throw obtuse, unseen challenges—how should you **solve problems** that you did not anticipate or have never encountered before?

A blindspot for **problem-solving** is that it often relies on its own internal, Linear, logic; trusting that the **solution** for the **problem** may be found within the system that created it. This logic often leads us to believe that **solutions** for all our **problems** are <u>fixed:</u> A faulty engine part <u>can only</u> be replaced with an identical part. A crossword solution <u>can only</u> have one correct answer.

Linear approaches to **problem-solving** are insufficient when:

   i: The problem is complex.
   ie: a doctor diagnosing a patient who feels 'sad'.

   ii: The problem is caused by the logic/system that created it.
   ie: productivity.

   iii: The problem is caused by a condition outside of its logic.
   ie: COVID19.

In environments with complex conditions, or where standard process has failed, you must often move outside the system from which the **problem** originated.

This is where creative skills like **adaptability** are useful for your mechanic: alternative engine parts may offer a suitable replacement (as suggested by Ferrucio Lamborghini).

And **emotional intelligence** is valuable for your doctor: understanding a patient's context is beneficial to diagnosis and treatment (as explained to our medical graduates).

Even crossword puzzles have been shown to offer **problem-solving** skills with **adaptable** value. During World War II, some savvy MI5 agent identified transferable traits of recognising patterns and deciphering clues and employed crossword experts to crack the German enigma code—a creative initiative that delivered critical insight and an Allied victory.

One of my favourite examples of complex problem-solving is Michael Burry's **proactive solution** to the Global Financial Crash of 2007… (I recommend watching the movie 'The Big Short'). Burry was a physician and hedge fund manager who found anomalies in the U.S mortgage bond markets.

Identifying that the system was due to fail, Burry invented an **original solution**. Burry invited banks to take his bet that surety of millions of mortgage bonds would fail, something that had never occurred in the entire history of Wall Street. (Note: this trade did not exist until Burry created it—to the banks, it was taking a sucker's money on a losing bet.)

Against every expert's advice, the history of Wall Street, and in the face of virulent investor hostility, Burry bet billions in client investment against the bedrock of American finance.
Burry won. The fallout was global, unprecedented and catastrophic... sound familiar?
This was a complex **problem** that could have been **solved** had a system not been so blindly trusted.

Burry's process wasn't divine intervention or genius—his Linear Expertise as a financial analyst recognised **problematic** symptoms: **i, ii,** and **iii.**

Burry's Creative Intelligence enabled him to **proactively adapt, innovate** and **compose** an **original solution.** Additionally he was **emotionally** secure enough to **risk** the backlash, endure the criticism and follow through.

Innovation

Improve existing systems, process, tools

(reactive/proactive)

2. Innovation: (reactive / proactive)

Improve existing tools, systems, process

What defines **innovation** is that it specifically relies upon an existing tool, system, service or concept. We most commonly observe this principle in the world of STEM where the development, implementation and improvement of tools/systems is a routine challenge.

As discussed in Chapter Two, we observe how neatly **innovation** is defined to align with **productivity**; at a societal level, law, education and medicine are all examples of foundational systems, constantly being adjusted, improved and updated. However, the skill of **innovation** is not inherent to Golden industries.

In the arts, your favourite band offering a cover version of an existing song demonstrates the principle of **innovation**; to take an existing concept, seek to enhance it, to deliver something new. Modern performances of Shakespeare, inherently require a degree of **innovation**. Shakespeare's plays were originally performed as pub-theatre. Shows ran close to four hours, as patrons ate, drank and chatted in the audience—the performance played out on stage, much like a 17th century soap opera.

Shakespeare performed today, must be **innovated** to be palatable for modern audiences; scripts are edited down to two hours, performances are **adapted** for modern themes and modern theatre audiences, who sit in solemn silence in enclosed auditoriums.

While **innovation** is a useful skill to understand, siloing out **innovative** process often proves to be as ineffective as it is expensive and time-consuming.

Independently, **innovation** has two Achilles' heels:

> **i:** If the dominant system is flawed, you are hopelessly bound to it. Much like **innovating** a legal system, structural change is incredibly slow and difficult.

> **ii:** When systems are interdependent, **innovation** disrupts the eco-system. Much like **innovating** one operating system, inadvertently creates a dozen separate 'unique features' network wide.

Successfully **innovating** complex, interdependent systems, requires a high-level of Creative Intelligence and similar to

problem-solving, the scope to think outside the primary system when it proves to be dysfunctional.

In practice, **innovation** has two modes, it is either **reactive** or **proactive**.

(Reactive) **innovation:**

Reactive innovation is the most common as people/ organisations have a difficult time justifying upgrades of systems, tools or process until they are suitably dysfunctional.
Then when competitor releases something new, we label it a 'disruption'.

Disruptive **innovation** forces you to **adapt**, but you are already behind the eight ball—consider the time, resources and investment organisations expend, only to play catch-up with a field that's already ahead of them.
They have set the tone, you are dancing to it as best you can.

For as long as you are **reactive**, you can never lead, in some industries, this is not an option, *ie:* Medicine. Military.
Ideally you would seek to shift your mindset and process to a **proactive** position.

(Proactive) **innovation:**

Proactive innovation enhances your service, uniquely positions you from competitors and establishes you as the 'Disruptor'.

Original innovation translates to 'key point of difference' and 'unique value proposition'.

You set the tone, it's your music they dance to.

Professional artistic practice demonstrates **proactive innovation**. Writers **proactively** draft, to sharpen their voice, and **compose original** stories.

Chefs **proactively** cook, to refine their palate, and **compose** new recipes.

Uber **proactively innovated** taxi services, to offer an **original** service.

PayPal **proactively innovated** payment gateways, for smoother, immediate transactions.

Each is an example of **proactive innovation**: how you can expand, enhance and refine your thinking, process and craft to deliver an **original** outcome as a unique artist and 'Disruptor'.

Composition

Arrange elements for optimal form + function

(proactive)

3. Composition: (proactive)

Arrange elements for optimal form + function

Composition is **proactive**; you're arranging elements to give something shape, form and function. **Composition** requires deliberate intention and may be found in aesthetics, in the design of UX and UI, and the arrangement of music, so let's start there.

Music is **composed**; musicians align specific notes to **compose** chords... Chords are **composed** to create melodies... Melodies are **composed** to create harmonies... Lyrics are **composed** to highlight the story.

Visually, **composition** exists in symmetry, it informs what we regard as beautiful.
We observe this in design: Lamborghini, Ferrari, Porsche, Aston Martin are all specifically engineered, **composed** to be dynamic, functional and pleasing to the eye.

A more technical example of **composition** is conditional logic. On a survey, do you need fifty individual Q&A data points? Or might you **compose** a few either/or options, to discern the information you'd like to elicit?

A chef demonstrates **composition** of flavours; selecting specific ingredients to season and enhance their meal and pays equal attention to the **composition**/the presentation on the plate.

Artists learn the rules of **composition** and equally demonstrate how to break them. Picasso's Weeping Woman displays zero symmetry, though the **composition** of lines, colour and texture is deliberate and emotive.

A simple exercise to develop **composition** as a skill is to **play** with LEGO. Yes, this is why LEGO is so often referenced in creative experiments; it is tangible, immediately accessible, requires no Linear Expertise, the outcomes are clearly observable and exercises may be applied to a group or an individual.

As an exercise if I gave you a tray full of random LEGO blocks, how would you **play** and what could you **compose**?
Would you tell a story...?
Order by colour...?
Design an abstract masterpiece...?
Or **compose** something structurally sound...?

- Challenge yourself to try each method.
- Challenge yourself to use minimal pieces.
- Challenge yourself to use all the pieces.
- Challenge yourself to unite all four approaches.

If you don't like it, knock it down and start again… you're just **playing**, it's not important. Music, cooking, building, LEGO, drawing or coding, **composition** is a universal creative skill.

Adaptability

Adapt intelligently to change /

Adopt alternative sources

(reactive / proactive)

4. Adaptability: (reactive / proactive)

React intelligently to change / Adopt alternative sources

Adaptability as a Creative Skill Set offers two modes, let us walk through **reactive** first.

(Reactive) **adaptability**

Generally in life, we are insulated from threat and disaster; there are rules, systems and processes that we can fall back on when catastrophe strikes, but what happens if the rules fail or cause us harm? How effectively do you **adapt** to circumstances outside of your control?

Adaptability is a trainable skill.
To develop our **adaptability**, we must position ourselves at the edge of 'the rules' to experience what may happen when they fail: it's in these moments that we learn to manage panic and **adapt** intelligently to take effective action.

Emergency services such as Fire, Police, Ambulance, Rescue regularly train **reactive adaptability:** teaching standard protocol and running 'disruptive' scenarios to simulate real life conditions.

So too, Armed Services; military professionalism involves strict control of the conditions within their influence and the capacity to **adapt** when these conditions shift... because they will shift.

Adaptability is often overlooked as a creative skill set creating a compound effect when we need it most.

How effectively did you **adapt** to COVID as a crisis?

Did you 'pivot' as a panic reflex?

Did you freeze and wait for the safety of the group?

Or could you **adapt** with an intelligent, specific purpose to achieve an optimal outcome?

More than a cognitive trait, adaptability is also an emotional response.

When you put faith in the comfort of 'the rules' you often ignore our more human **emotional** impulses when life goes awry.

In the shock of a break-up, are you always so clear headed to follow your five-step exit strategy?

When your employer decides you're redundant, does your attitude remain professional?

Your **emotional** ability to **adapt** intelligently to shock, change or crises is a skill that you can hone and cultivates your ability to clearly assess **risk**, to mitigate it when necessary, to step into it when required.

Reactive adaptability in Gold allows you to **problem-solve** faster and more effectively; it facilitates **innovation** and is of massive value in operational roles where there are live conditions.

Reactive adaptability in Rouge allows actors to improvise, musicians to perform jazz and dancers to swing in rhythm with a partner.
There are 'rules' to improvisation, jazz and swing—artists **play** in, out and around the rules, dynamically **adapting** in the moment.

(Proactive) **adaptability**

Proactive adaptability allows you to observe references outside of your sphere and **adapt** what you need for your own purposes.
Proactive adaptability allows you to ask:

We do this our way, how do other people do this?

Could we **adapt** this? Why/why not?

Proactive adaptability proves exceptionally valuable when applied to **innovation** and **problem-solving**.

Uber, (founded in 2009) **adapted** the digital platform of Airbnb (founded 2008).

Consumer + Third-party Platform = Service provider
Guest + (Airbnb) = Accommodation service
Passenger + (Uber) = Ride-sharing service

The same model **adapted** for alternative services, has since been **adapted** worldwide for a variety of purposes.

Proactive adaptability also aligns with creative skills such as **composition** and **originality**.

Artists are notorious thieves: in Rouge we refer to **adapted** sources as 'influences'. Observing something shiny in another world, an artist will **proactively adapt** it to **innovate** and/or **compose** something **original**.

This is what Austin Kleon meant when he recommended we 'steal like an artist'. However this sentiment is all too often taken at face value and abused as a hack by those lacking Linear Expertise or **originality**.

Constantly **adapting** influences from elsewhere neuters your creative development—you're limited and derivative, unable to think, **compose** or **innovate** for yourself.

You're a parrot mimicking phrases or another Uber knock-off.

The films of Quentin Tarantino are a more accurate example of how to successfully **adapt** influences.

Students of film will recognise elements of grind house, horror, western, Hong Kong chop-socky, Kurosawa and 70's blaxploitation—independently, each element contradicts the other in style, tone and function.

Tarantino's goal is not to gather pretty things like a crow—the goal is tell a particular story—he **adapts** dialogue, themes, camera angles, even font styles, that are dynamic, effective and serve the story—weaving them seamlessly into an iconic, **original** style of storytelling.

Tarantino himself has become an influential style to be emulated.

Emotional Intelligence (E.Q)

Empathetic understanding /

Ability to interpret context

(reactive/proactive)

5. E.Q: (reactive / proactive)

Empathetic understanding / Ability to interpret context

Emotional intelligence (E.Q) is commonly discussed as empathy, however its potential and application is much more significant than this. **E.Q** is the basis of human connection; it is an unconscious contract of 'do you see me... do you accept me'? From understanding how another person may feel in a relationship, to the value of ethics within society, some of the greatest social and political revolutions have been driven by the need to improve the quality of life for others.

(Reactive) **emotional intelligence**

Reactive E.Q is employed by (good) counsellors, psychologists, managers, parents, humans. They can listen and process another's emotions with objectivity and compassion, without feeling attacked, offended or becoming reactionary.

E.Q helps us establish foreign context; it's an understanding that our internal world may not be another's internal world, there may be other perspectives to consider... what might they be?

This ability to interpret foreign contexts is not limited to people and emotions. We observe **C7** employ this skill to recognise the Hotel Room within its natural context; this insight allowed her to achieve an optimal outcome.

This ability to understand and establish alternative contexts is of significant value in fields such as data-analytics and statistical analysis. Data points are useful, though understanding where data has come from, from whom, why it was obtained and the contextual conditions that influence your findings, is of significantly greater value.

(Proactive) **emotional intelligence**

Proactive E.Q is most observable within the Arts.
To intimately connect with another human requires a deep, mature, refined sense of **E.Q**.
Artists, through their medium, **proactively** demonstrate the power, potential and potency of human connection, often able to articulate complex, unspoken emotions with crystalline clarity.

Authors **proactively** flex **E.Q** to **compose** realistic characters; this process allows you to **play** with how your hero might think, believe, fear, love; this will inform how they speak, how they act, the relationships they form and the risks they're willing to take to achieve their goal.

An actor's process is both **reactive** and **proactive.**
Actors **reactively** flex their **E.Q** to 'get inside the mind' of the written character, understand their motivations and relationships; then **proactively** flex their **E.Q** to embody this **emotional** state and realistically bring the character to life.
Singers employ a similar skill to interpret lyrics and harmony, translate it in a way to bring **emotional** truth to the story and **compose** an **original** performance.

When **E.Q** is applied **proactively** as a collective, we found social initiatives and charities. We understand that our circumstances may not be equivalent to others' and we seek to cultivate equity, to build a society where all may thrive. Diversity and inclusion, fair trade and ethical business practices are all **emotionally** driven initiatives, key to sustainable cultures and humane economics.

Originality

Creation of something new, not a replica

(proactive)

6. Originality: (proactive)

Creation of something new, not a replica

Linear Expertise can carry you quite far but, in every industry, there is one element that separates the good, from the exceptional —**originality**—and is perhaps my favourite, since it arrives via the opposite pathway of what we observe.

When we talk of **original** concepts, we commonly think of 'Eureka' moments—lightning strikes, Muses kiss us, there is divine inspiration and magical ideas come to life!

However, in order to create anything new, you require an informed opinion of what has come before you. It is this ethic of curiosity that prompts deeper research of your subject, to critical evaluate what already exists and encourages exploration of what is yet unknown… this is where we discover truly genuine, **original** insight.

Two friends stranded in Paris at night, unable to hail a cab…
EUREKA!
Uber was born.
Great story. Succinct. Powerful. Observing the behemoth that Uber has become, they must be geniuses.

The reality is, two founders, Travis Kalanick and Garret Camp, had each sold their tech start-ups the year prior and were in Paris for a conference. While a seed may have been planted that winter's night... exactly nothing came of it.

Over a year later, Kalanick and Camp would reconnect on this concept (the initial idea was for a limousine service). It was a further year still, of negotiation, research, development and raising capital before the first Uber ride was booked in San Francisco in 2010.

I draw on Uber specifically because the concept is not new. Ride-sharing has existed since the horse and carriage. Parents and co-workers carpool daily.
The logic of creating a car service—with no actual cars—to compete in a world of taxis, hire cars, limousines and public transport, seemed absurd.

It was their relative Linear Expertise within tech start-ups and VC funding, that Camp and Kalanick were able to **compose** a platform, **innovate** and offer ride-sharing in an **original** way.

Originality is **proactive**—you move from relying on the crowd to stepping out and claiming new space by offering something unique.

In **Gold**, this principle of **originality** is how you define your 'key point of difference'.

In **Rouge**, the ethic of **originality** is commonly intuitive—we don't want to be like anyone else and this is where I advise caution...

Prioritising **originality** over form, function or purpose, is a recipe for disaster; just because something is **original** doesn't mean it is good, useful or of benefit.

Artists are particularly guilty of this sin—'passion' or 'personality' is not a substitute for Linear Expertise in any field, and while art may be subjective to taste, it may also be objectively critiqued.

While the belief that everyone is creative and has a right to express themselves, may be valid—this should not be conflated to mean, every expression is **original** or worth the price of admission.

Much of art is self-indulgent masturbation.

We've all seen it. I've undoubtedly performed it.

Original ≠ good, useful, effective

Likewise we should not conflate every new product to be original or necessary—a bias marketers exploit to full potential.

Apple releases a new i-Phone every year.
Is it useful? Yes.
Is it **innovative**? Advertisers claim it to be so.
Is it **original**? Not really, one might pause to ask, is it any more useful, **innovative** or **original** than last years model?

I once saved a government organisation $27 million by using this logic to explain how their new **innovative** system, was a larger version of Apple's I-Phone... a product anyone can buy, that does not provide any **original** competitor advantage.

Genuine **original** insight that is of practical value, is facilitated via deep research and critical reflection. It is more effective as a by-product or seasoning to a project, rather than its goal.
Originality encourages you to be curious, to search, to question, to push the needle and demands **proactive** attention.
In short, **originality** is how you define yourself and lead (provided you've put the work in).

Conclusion

Summary

This is a breakdown of the Six Creative Skill Sets, as an overview, you should be able to:

1: Identify what creative strengths you already have.

2: Identify how these skills apply to your Linear Expertise.

3: Validate creative process/potential and creative outcomes.

4: Recognise how these traits are versatile and interdependent.

What defines **optimal** creative outcomes and positions you as a **proactive**, prolific leader is...

5: Your Linear Expertise + Six Creative Skill Sets.

LINEAR + CREATIVE = OPTIMAL OUTCOMES

The Six Creative Skill Sets are the foundation of creative thinking, process and outcomes.

They are universal; they are not exclusive to any personality, nor beholden to any profession.

You can develop these skills for yourself, right now, they are not dependent on budget, tools, collaboration or location.

There is no rigid framework, no subscription, no-one need give you permission, you only need to take ownership for yourself.

Your creative potential is unlimited and entirely in your hands.

*

How can you start now?

There are three simple steps you can take now to get you started.

1. Identify the skill you wish to develop.
2. Select whether it is **reactive** or **proactive**.
3. **Play** with subjects that flex the skills you wish to develop.

When you're starting out, remember the creative concept of **play**: exploration without attachment to outcome.

This may feel difficult in the beginning: when learning a new language; initially we feel awkward, foreign and uncomfortable.

There is no right or wrong way to **play**, though I will offer one suggestion…

To develop a skill like **composition** does not mean you have to become an illustrator—there is little value in 'drawing to be creative' if you don't like, need or want to draw.

Similarly, keeping a journal is popular advice, but it is not a prop that will *make you* creative.

I encourage you to **compose** in ways that are of interest to you and/or relevant to your Linear Expertise—you will find it more relevant, more satisfying and you will notice improvement sooner.

If you're an engineer, **play** with **composition** of design and **play** with different math to build it.

If you're a chef, **play** with **composition** of flavours and different **compositions** on the plate.

If you're feeling brave, **play** with skills that will develop your creativity in abstract methods.

Pick up that long lost musical instrument, (re)learn the Linear Expertise and **play** with **composition, emotional intelligence,** and **originality,** all at once.

*

I often **play** with card magic, to sharpen the following skills:

Problem-solving: to troubleshoot my own handling.
Innovation: to enhance standard effects in my own way.
Composition: to polish presentation and craft new routines.
Adaptability: to borrow elements of performance.
EQ: to put myself in the mind of the spectator.
Originality: to develop my own handlings and routines

Card tricks or consulting, how will you draw out **original** results? Mechanics or medicine, how will you **problem-solve** effectively? Acting or architecture, how will you **innovate** and **compose** with standard resources?

The Six Creative Skill Sets are what you need to develop—skills that exist outside of technical learning—that harmonise and enhance your Linear Expertise.

The reveal

Pick a card...

Remember in the Introduction I promised you a magic trick? Here's where I walk you through the reveal....

There is a **problem**, a challenge, a critical demand for creativity. What is it, how did we get here, how can we develop it ourselves? It is a complex **problem** with many subjective conditions.

The dominant model of defining creativity as a Golden or psychological process is limited and inaccurate; standard process to produce creative results is ineffective and inconsistent. I identified a **problem** with conditions **i, ii, iii.**

By moving outside of standard frameworks, I demonstrated an abundance of creative potential that lies outside of scientific rationale: that your creativity behaves more as a language you can learn and that you may develop it via specific skills, rather than relying on quirks of personality.

I **proactively innovated, adapted** and **composed** a comprehensive **solution** to satisfy multiple complex conditions.

Identifying creative behaviour as both **reactive/proactive** and distilling six specific skills, offers a clear, practical guide that you can begin to apply immediately.

The Six Creative Skill Sets was **composed** to offer clarity, form and function to creativity, to help train creative process and craft optimal creative outcomes. They also serves as a framework to vet ideas, solutions and products against, to assess their creative integrity and value.

To make my case I **proactively adapted** examples from education, philosophy, art, history, theatre, business, film, algebra, relationships, science/technology, cooking, language, psychology, Shakespeare, sleight of hand card magic and my own life experience.

Emotional Intelligence enables me to identify with you, the audience, wanting to understand creativity but perhaps not quite 'getting it'... yet.

To identify with you, the professional, who understands the value in qualitative, divergent, atypical, creative thinking and the necessity to apply it on command, reliably and effectively.

It allowed me to be vulnerable and share some of my own process and insecurities with you; I've no need to fear judgement or retribution, it is not a legitimate **risk**.

Emotional Intelligence supported my resilience to persevere and complete this book—to spend nine months writing a first draft during COVID, to offer it to an editor, to be told...

'this isn't a book'... and to start again from scratch.

The humility to accept, not that I couldn't write, but that I lacked the Linear Expertise to structure prose for a business, thought leadership book. To sit and redraft for another year and finally self-publish—all in all, a total of two-and-a-half years.

I used **Abstract Intelligence** to invent Gold and Rouge as metaphors for you to identify with.

The analogy of 'creativity as a language' provides clarity and context to the **problem** of translation—how architects and dancers may each speak this language (or not).

This metaphor articulates the clash between corporate and the arts—how productivity as a model is non-conducive and why scientific study struggles to glean an accurate translation.

That this language is not a gift from Muses or unique to eccentric personalities, that you can learn it, develop your fluency and switch to this 'bilingual mode', on command.

What I offer is an **original** theory, **original** insight and an **original** framework, that I believe can be of significant benefit.

Was it luck that all of these elements mysteriously fell into place? Is it divine inspiration that blessed me? Did I randomly connect things or steal like an artist? Like all good magic tricks, the technique is hidden and what is produced is a unique effect. What you observe is a book... what you don't immediately see is the process to deliver the outcome: over twenty years of Linear Expertise, **professional** artistic practice and corporate contracts, aligned with **proactive** application of Six Creative Skill Sets.

Linear Expertise + Six Creative Skill Sets

As you draw back this curtain you realise, there is no such thing as magic, only knowledge, discipline and skill—that impossible is within your reach and extraordinary may be crafted by those with vision.

This book is Applied Creativity.

Contact +

Resources

Backwards isn't an option...

The demand for creativity is not a passing fad, I anticipate it will get worse before it gets better.
Change is often slow; cultures resist conditions until catastrophe. Productivity is gripped tighter than ever as leadership seek to wrest control during disruption.

By reading this book, you're already ahead of the curve by recognising what's needed, why, and how you can **proactively** develop your creative intelligence.

For some guidance into your professional creative development, there are a few ways I can help you:

1. I offer executive coaching to develop your creative skill sets.

2. I host workshops/keynotes for teams invested in optimal creative process.

3. I independently advise boards + consult on select projects.

As a Strategic Consultant, my expertise lies in designing **Force Multipliers** - www.cssellers.com/casestudies

Force Multipliers are:
- Single solutions.
- That satisfy multiple complex conditions.
- Move your organisation from a **reactive** to **proactive** position.
- Incur minimal cost/risk.
- Deliver an **optimal** outcome.

Recently I offered Netflix a **Force Multiplier** to reposition itself as the world's leading streaming service: a strategy that opens up and diversifies new revenue streams, incurs zero risk, requires zero additional investment and doesn't require them to advertise.

You can review it here: www.cssellers.com/post/how-i-d-fix-netflix-overnight

Contact + Resources

If you found this book interesting, I'd love to hear from you:

Website: www.cssellers.com

Email: christopher@cssellers.com

LinkedIn: linkedin.com/in/c-s-sellers

YouTube: www.youtube.com/@christophers.sellers

Some articles I've written on creative process that may interest you…

'It is the Artist who Paints - why AI will never replace us'

A breakdown of creative AI and the difference between the tradesman and their tools.

'How I'd Fix Netflix Overnight'

My creative strategy to reposition Netflix as the premier streaming service, a Force Multiplier that opens up new revenue, doesn't require them to advertise, incurs zero risk and is free.

'How a deck of playing cards can improve your creativity'

How your ability to control and manipulate the 52 factorial unlocks limitless potential.

'How to get a coconut out of a tree'

When standard tools and process are insufficient, how can you flex your creativity to adapt, solve, innovate… eat coconuts?

Find more articles, art + insight at:

www.cssellers.com/cssellersblog

Acknowledgments

To my family who've endured a misfit inspired to change the world, who supported my idealism through pandemics and a variety of catastrophes, thank you for your patience.

To my peers, Robert Anderson, Sharee Johnson, Adrian Jobson, Sarah Bass, and Kelly Irving who pooled us together, thank you for your friendship, guidance and encouragement.

To all the Members of our Radically Creative (Impossible) Book Launch and the Contributors who built this hype train: Travis Hinkle, Tiffany Redden and Mathilde Bernard Funderburk, your selfless contribution is a debt I shall forever owe… if you ever need a favour, call me first.
To read all about this project: www.cssellers.com/hypetrain

To every drama teacher I had through high-school (all women), you saved my adolescence.

To Adrian Barnes who dared me to 'never stop writing' and Linda Nicholls-Gidley who challenged me to find and use my own voice, I carry both your teaching and wisdom with me to this day.

To you, the reader, the brave one who dared to think differently, to challenge convention, question the status quo and chose to think for yourself—I extend my thanks and sincerest support.

The potential to create all change, lies in you.

- Christopher

Christopher describes his career as…

"Fifteen years of hopscotch between corporate and creative".

A consultant, speaker and founder of the Six Creative Skill Sets, Christopher is also a professional actor, screenwriter, playwright, street photographer, is conversational in French and Japanese, can tap dance, perform card magic and has a strong tenor range…because Rouge is equally valuable.

Christopher's revolutionary model of Applied Creativity + Six Creative Skill Sets offers organisations a breakthrough framework to practically develop creative thinking, skills and process for optimal outcomes.

Christopher lives in Sydney, Australia, drinks espresso daily, consults for clients globally, speaks on creativity frequently and is looking forward to travelling internationally, imminently.

For more information: www.cssellers.com

Lightning Source UK Ltd.
Milton Keynes UK
UKHW021520100223
416667UK00012B/622